Mrs. Wistrom's ABCs

What I Learned
Raising Three All-Americans

by

Kathy Sasse Wistrom

Stellar Press
St. Louis, Missouri
www.BooksOnStLouis.com

Mrs. Wistrom's ABCs

by Kathy Sasse Wistrom
© Copyright 2001 by Kathy Sasse Wistrom
All rights reserved

ISBN   0-9708422-2-8

Printed in the United States of America

Published and distributed by:

Stellar Press
1524 S. Big Bend Blvd., Second Floor
St. Louis, Missouri 63117
877-572-8835 (toll-free)
www.BooksOnStLouis.com
e-mail: info@BooksOnStLouis.com

To Mr. Hough's
Fourth Grade
Class #

Enjoy!

Kathy Bostrom

'53

Dedication

This book is dedicated to the men in my life who encouraged me to fulfill my dream: Ron, Chance, Grant, & Tracey.

Brad Haugh
8330 E. Quincy Ave.
#F303
Denver, CO 80237

Grant, Tracey, Ron and Chance at Chance's wedding.

Introduction

I am not presumptious enough to tell you that my husband, Ron, and I have been perfect parents or that our children, Chance, Grant and Trace, are God's gifts to the world. I don't consider myself an authority on child psychology. This book resulted from comments that were made to me on various trips to Nebraska to watch my sons play footabll. I love to tell stories about the boys, and people are always asking me about the Huskers or the Rams. Several women suggested that I should write a book about our experiences with the boys; how all three managed to get college scholarships or what it was like watching Grant play in his first NFL game.

As more people mentioned the idea, Ron encouraged me to do it! He knows that I love to write, and when the boys heard what I was considering, they jumped on the bandwagon. Since I'm always telling the boys to aim for their goals, they told me to put my money where my mouth was!

From then on, every time I would see one of the boys, they'd ask about the book. When Grant said he had met several publishers who were interested, I had to finish it. I also knew that even if it didn't sell many copies, at least I've put some of my thoughts on paper. As forgetful as I'm getting, that would be a big plus!

Although, I have many more stories I could tell about the boys, I tried to write about what we did that may have helped them become successful football players as well as good, young men. Again, I don't claim to know everything, but I do believe that because of our experiences with coaches, colleges, agents, etc., we may have some helpful suggestions. If nothing else, at least my story may make you feel better about your own kids. You'll find out, just as I did, that the people you see on TV are pretty much just like your own children with the same problems, dreams, disappointments, etc.

Maybe you'll laugh at some of the stories and sympathize with others. More importantly, I hope you see yourself or your husband and kids in the pages.

And I hope you learn from either what we did that was right or what we did that was wrong.

This book has been a labor of love. Thank you for reading it.

And may you always take Chances,
Have your wishes Granted,
And find a Trace of happiness in all you do!

(I sent that as a Christmas card one year)

Kathy Sasse Wistrom, 2001

Mrs. Wistrom's ABCs

What I Learned
Raising Three All-Americans

by

Kathy Sasse Wistrom

Stellar Press - St. Louis, Missouri
www.BooksOnStLouis.com

Our Three Sons

All three of our boys, Chance, Grant, and Tracey, have different personalities. What worked for one didn't work for the others. We could always just look at Chance, and if he knew we were disappointed in him, then that was punishment enough. Grant, on the other hand, needed physical punishment for him to know just what we expected of him. Tracey usually seemed to know what was the right thing for him to do. He didn't

Chance, Grant, Tracey

want to be corrected with either a look or a touch of the hand. You could gently remind him. But we didn't learn this over night. It was basically trial and error!

In The Beginning

As the first born, Chance has always been the one the others turned to for advice. Although both Grant and Trace played football at bigger colleges, Chance is the one who started the whole thing, and his "little" brothers consider that he is the expert. Both boys attribute a great deal of their success to Chance. They watched him develop work ethics, and they learned from him. They saw him overcome obstacles to achieve success, and even today they know how hard he works to be the best he can be.

I often refer to Chance as my "broken plate" child. You know how it is when you serve a large dinner, and someone always has to have the chipped plate. Chance always seems to get the broken plate. If something was going to happen to one of the boys, it always seemed to happen to Chance. He would be the one to stop and help a little old lady on the side of the road only to have three thugs jump out of the bushes to rob him! (This didn't really happen, but I think you get the picture.)

When he was on the all-star baseball team in Florida, he would get up to the plate ready to bat and a sudden downpour would occur. The weekend that Grant was drafted, someone broke into Chance's house. When we lived in Florida, he and his dad worked

Chance and the Nova

on a restoring a Chevy Nova for three years. When others were going to the beach or movies, Chance would be sanding, welding, etc. In the move back to Missouri, we transported the Nova in a moving van because it had just been painted. When the door to the van was opened, we found that a huge beam had fallen from the ceiling of the van onto Chance's "pride and joy." During a college football game, he ran 85 yards for a touchdown (which is the height of a defensive end's career) only to find the touchdown would be called back. Things like that have just been a part of Chance's life. I always tell him that "adversity builds character." Finally Chance started telling me that he felt like he'd had enough character building, and it was time that Grant and Tracey had some. I would also tell him that God always had a plan for his life, and everything that happens leads to this plan. After one good samaritan stop where he lost his contact lenses, he told me that he thought God should reevaluate his plan!

Chance (right) and his Cousin Brian

But whatever God's plan, Chance has had to suffer through our plans. As the first born, he experienced all the first time parenting syndrome. He had all the "new stuff." We just knew that if we followed the baby book he'd be perfect. The truth is babies need to be fed, changed, and loved and they still aren't perfect.

Chance was a beautiful little boy with blonde hair, blue eyes, and dimples. Put this atop a pudgy body, and you have the Gerber baby. As a laid-back person, I wasn't obsessed about when the boys walked or talked. In fact, the only thing I remember is that the boys wore diapers until they could almost change themselves. They took bottles until they were nearly two years old. I was determined they wouldn't have pacifiers, but we carried a bottle everywhere we went!

Chance probably had the most pressure put on him. We had more time to devote to him, and we wanted what all parents want - a perfect child! We expected him to be the best he could be, academically and athletically.

In a sense, we grew-up as Chance grew-up. We learned he would push us as far as we allowed. If we picked him up from his bed after ten minutes of crying, then he'd cry longer the next time. Eventually, although it broke my heart, we just let him cry himself to sleep. Although he held on to my leg and cried hysterically when I left him at daycare, I learned he'd stop the minute the door was closed. We learned we couldn't protect him from getting hurt, but we could help him deal with the hurt. When he fell, he had to get up and try again. Children have to be exposed to failure because life is filled with such situations, and if we never let them face failure when they're young, then it's even more devastating when they become adults.

Of all the boys, Chance is probably the most tenacious because he has faced more controversy in his life. As a mother it breaks my heart to see him or any of the boys struggle against injustices they don't deserve. However, that's why we have to teach our children to handle these situations and face them head-on.

Chance was a delight to raise. He always wanted to do the right thing, make us proud. He is very loving and compassionate. He tries to do what's right, although it sometimes backfires. Once he volunteered to ring the bell for the Salvation Army, and his relief never arrived so instead of being there two hours, he was there about five. With his busy schedule as a coach and teacher, he volunteered to help with troubled youth, only to be told that THEY thought he wouldn't have time to attend the adult meetings. (I would think they'd want anyone of Chance's caliber if they had time to work with the boys, and forget the adult meetings!)

After getting a BS in Industrial Hygiene, he realized what he really wanted to do was work with young people, so he went back to school, got a teaching degree, and he is currently the AD/assistant principal/head football coach at Seneca, Missouri. He loves what he's doing because he loves kids. I can say without any doubt he will be the best coach a player could have because he'll be fair and honest. He's been where they are. I'm not sure parents will always agree with his choice of players, but again I'm sure if you ask the kids, they will agree with Coach Wistrom's plan.

As a child, Chance was very stubborn (my word choice) or independent (his grandmother, Gammy's word choice). Even today, he has very strong convictions about his beliefs. Like his dad, Ron, he says what he means, and he has little patience for others who don't. Along the same line, he is a very loyal person. If he believes in you or your idea, he'll go to war with you. If he believes a certain boy should play at a certain position, that's where he'll play despite who his parents are. As a teacher myself, I worry about him because teaching is not what it was when I began. There's far too much parental and government interference in the schools today, and it's not always supportive. I just hope Chance doesn't get discouraged because he is the kind of young man the teaching profession needs.

I used to refer to Chance as "poor Chance" until Ron reminded me of my own psychology. If a child hears something enough, he believes it. Ron also reminded me that Chance is doing exactly what he wants to do. He has a job he loves. He lives in a small community close to fishing and hunting, which was always his dream. He works with people he admires and respects and who have become his friends. He's close enough to us where

Dee and Chance

he and his wife, Dee, can see us when THEY want, but we're far enough away that I can't interfere (not very easily, anyway!). He gets to watch his brothers play football on national TV.

And most importantly, he has an adorable wife who shares his love for football, the outdoors, and family and friends.

At the next family dinner, maybe I'll make sure he gets a new plate!!

In The Middle

Grant was supposed to be our girl. I always thought that if you were a good person, God just give you what you wanted. We had wanted to have a boy, followed by a girl. We had the boy and we were ready for the girl. At the time, I had read a Life magazine article about what a couple could do to help determine the sex of their child. (I won't go into details, but if you're interested the article is somewhere in the 1975 series.)

And despite what they say, just ask Ron Wistrom, girls are harder to get than boys. Or there is another possibility, perhaps more believable. It could be that I just didn't read the article very carefully, and I got the "directions" confused. According to Ron the second possibility is FAR more believable. Or perhaps a Wistrom girl just wasn't part of God's plan. So there I was all prepared for a girl, and this ten-pound boy arrived.

When Grant was born, I actually cried because he was a boy. The nurse comforted me by saying that since boys were harder to raise, when God found a good mother for boys, he gave her all she could handle. Good story, huh?

I didn't really have any names for boys. Remember, I knew he'd be a girl, so I had names like Liberty Lee and Shay Dee ready. Ron's mother always said that's why God didn't give me a girl. He couldn't bear to see a little girl with those names. On the way to the hospital we decided on Grant since it was July 3, 1976, the bicentennial year.

Grant was a sickly baby from the day he was born. I often worried that perhaps my disappointment could have been a part of his problem.

I should have known Grant would have problems because the day that he was born was like Noah's flood. We were living down the road from where we live now, and it had rained for two days. Not only was the bridge covered, but also the entire valley down from our house was covered with water. At one point, we thought Grant would be delivered at home. Since that day, Grant's life has been anything but normal.

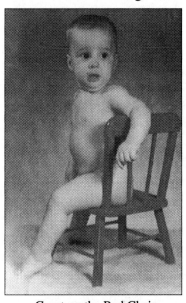

Eventually we found out that he was allergic to everything, and everything irritated his stomach; therefore, he reacted like people who had ulcers. He threw up like Linda Blair in The Exorcist. He cried constantly, and he never slept. No one could hold him except me, my neighbor Louise, or his Gammy. Where Chance looked like a poster boy

Grant on the Red Chair

for Gerber commercials, Grant looked like a refugee from a third world country. At one of the Ram's games, they showed a picture of Grant on the big screen as part of their "Guess the Player" portion. In the picture Grant is sitting naked on a little red chair. Of course he took a lot of teasing about the picture.

The truth is that I don't really have any baby pictures of Grant because we could never get one taken before he threw up all over everything. I got that picture because after changing him into three clean suits, I stripped him down, sat him in the little chair, and barked at the frustrated photographer, "Just take the picture!!" It's become one of my favorites. Of course, it's one of the few baby pictures I have of Grant.

Finally, when Grant was about four months old, he slept through the night. I was so excited that I was afraid to go into his room for fear I'd wake him. When I finally tiptoed in, my heart sank. He had thrown up all over his crib, and he was covered from head to toe with it and diarrhea! I must have been in shock, because I very calmly scooped him up and took him to the bathroom to wash him. At that point I lost it. When I turned on the water, red clay came out of the faucet! I became hysterical. I just sat down and bawled. All the while, Grant was still sleeping which should have been a clue that something was seriously wrong.

I called Ron at work, and he called his folks and asked them to drive-up from Grove, Oklahoma. I called the doctor at the hospital. When I described how lethargic Grant was, he told me to bring him to the hospital immediately. By that time, everyone had arrived and Ron's step-dad suggested we contact Ron's uncle who was a doctor at Kansas University Medical Center in Kansas City. After talking to our local doctor, he suggested we leave immediately for Kansas City because they would be able to run tests and get the results more quickly than Joplin, even considering the drive from Webb City. I still don't understand why he didn't suggest we take an ambulance. Anyway, Grandpa drove like a man possessed hoping we'd get stopped and perhaps get a police escort. Wouldn't you know it, there wasn't a policeman in sight.

Grant never awoke during the entire trip. We talked about unimportant issues because we were all thinking the same thing, this little guy was probably dying in our arms.

When we arrived, nurses rushed out and immediately started him with IVs. As they scooped him out of my arms, Grant released a slimy green gelatin-like fluid. At the time, I had no idea that people often release such fluids when they die. The emergency room doctor said if we would have had to take the time to fill out papers, he would have died.

The doctors discovered that Grant had infantile botulism, a very rare disease. We were fortunate that one of the doctors who was called in to examine Grant was familiar with the diagnosis, because at that time there were very few diagnosed cases in the United States. The disease can take a life so quickly because it is actually in the bloodstream. I should really be grateful to our local doctor, because I'm sure our hospital would not have been able to diagnose it and treat it so quickly. The doctors in Kansas City said it's unusual for babies to get the disease, because it has to get to the bloodstream. In Grant's case, they assume he was infected through his baby shots, although it can't be proven.

Whatever the cause, it made me wonder if other children have died from this, but the reasons were never known. We were just very fortunate that everything worked out as it did. What about the clay in our well water which was what pushed me over the edge? Ron did everything to find out what had caused that to happen, and he never could find any other problems. We had our well checked, and it has never happened since then. The well is still working today.

So, what did cause chunks of clay to come out at that particular time and place? In my opinion, it was a part of God's plan. Had that not happened, I would have cleaned Grant, put him back to bed, and thanked God that he was finally sleeping. A coincidence? I don't think so. I call it a miracle. I don't want Grant to ever forget this story because it should remind him that God does have big plans for him. God spared him for a reason, and he needs to make sure that he never takes anything for granted.

What else happened as a result of our visit to the KU Medical Center? The doctors also discovered that Grant was allergic to all milk products, even soybean products, goat's milk, wheat products, and more. They put him on a formula called Neutramagen which cost about $100 a case, and a case lasted about one week. Grant was the million-dollar baby! But it worked; Grant began growing and thriving, and you know what he looks like today. Ron would like to find out if other children on the formula developed as Grant did.   If so, he's determined to have our grandchildren on it. (Neutramagen makers, remember I'm available for commercials!)

Grant in Florida

Just because he began to eat and sleep does not mean Grant became the perfect baby. He was not always as interested in pleasing us as his brother was.   Where Chance wouldn't want to upset his dad, Grant would weigh the consequences and see if the crime was worth the punishment. If it were, he'd try to get away with it. But, he always knew if he got caught he had to pay the price.   Grant learned not to question the punishment. He knew he'd done wrong, so he'd pay the piper.

Chance lulled us into a false security about our child-rearing techniques.   We truly never worried about Chance making stupid decisions. I will admit that today we are learning that Chance didn't always do the right thing; he just didn't get caught. On the other hand, Grant always seemed to be in the middle of things. He marched to a different drummer. He always had his own ideas about doing things, and he usually thought his ideas were better than ours. When it came to sports, Chance thought his dad knew everything. At seven years old, Grant told his Gammy, "If my dad knew as much about football as he thought he did, he'd be pretty good." Gammy reminded Grant that if he valued his life, he'd keep that comment to himself.

Because of that personality trait, Grant wasn't always ready to do everything Ron told him to do, especially when it came to football. When Ron talked to Chance about his performance or told him he was disappointed in his playing, Chance would assure Ron he'd make him proud; he'd be the best he could be. Ron tried that with Grant, and one day when Ron was using this psychology it backfired.

Grant was about eight years old playing Pop Warner football in Florida. I can still see that curly little blonde head pretending he was absorbing every word Ron said. Ron told him that he thought Grant should be embarrassed about his lack of hustle and effort. He went on to say that perhaps Grant should go to his room and think about his football career. After all, there wasn't any point for Grant or Ron to be embarrassed about Grant's playing. Maybe he should just look for something else. And Grant agreed to go to his room to ponder his decision as Ron smiled smugly about his parenting skills.

Of course Chance would have returned to promise his dad that he would make him proud, and Ron expected the same from Grant. WRONG! Whatever Grant was doing in his room, I don't think he was thinking about his dad's disappointment.

Grant came bouncing out, climbed up into Ron's lap, looked up with those big blue eyes, and spoke the unspeakable: "Dad, you're right. There's no point in you being embarrassed, so I'll just quit." He kissed his dad, bounced off the chair, and decided his days of hot practices were over.

I waited for the loud roar, but Ron was cool. As his veins pulsed in his neck, he caught Grant before he made it to the door, and he calmly told him that he had rethought the situation. Grant needed to learn an important rule; you never quit in the middle of the game. So, no, Grant wouldn't quit in the middle of the season. He didn't have to play next year, but he couldn't quit now. Ron continued that perhaps he (Ron) hadn't made the right evaluation. Maybe Grant needed more sleep or shouldn't be running around as much and perhaps that would improve his performance. Needless to say, Grant never mentioned quitting again.

Ron and I both learned an important lesson, also. No two children are alike, and there's no assurance that what works for one will work for the other. We could often make Chance feel guilty about what he'd done. Guilt didn't work with Grant. Where Chance liked to stay at home, Grant would go with anyone at anytime. Where Chance always gets hyper before a game by listening to rock music,

Grant dreaming of football

Grant will often take a nap on the bench right before entering the field. This really does drive Ron nuts!!

While Chance could work for hours on a project he liked, Grant couldn't sit still. Grant was like an accident looking for a place to happen. During his sophomore year of high school, he and Chance and their cousin, Brian, were working on a Ford Bronco they were restoring. Somehow, Grant managed to set fire to the backyard, break Ron's welder, and punch a hole in the wall. Grant told Ron the backyard just went up and when he threw water on it, it got worse. He punched the hole in the wall because it was that or punch Tracey. (He did fix the hole where Ron would have never noticed it, but Grant admitted to it anyway.) But he forgot about the welder. It was an accident, but later when Ron went to use it and found it broken, Grant was punished all over again. The accident would have been forgiven, but forgetting to mention it was a big mistake. So Grant was basically grounded for most of the summer. And grounded meant grounded. I hated it because I was home and I had to see that it was enforced. I felt as if I were grounded, also! Coach Thompson joked that Grant was the only kid who was excited about two-a-days because he got to see him friends!

Grant's life continued this way. I hate to admit it, but when someone said Chance had done something, I'd say, "Are you sure? That doesn't sound like Chance?" On the other hand, when they said it about Grant, I'd say, "What did he do?"

Still Grant was, and is, a delightful kid. He's funny, and he doesn't mind laughing at himself. He's very kind and compassionate. He has a sincere concern for those less fortunate. One of his main charities, Grant's Circle of Friends, involves working with kids with cancer. When he's with them, he's a little boy all over again. He will do anything for kids.

Now he doesn't have a lot of patience with adults. He'll always sign autographs for kids, but sometimes I feel that he's too impatient with adults; however, seeing more and more of Grant's autographs being sold on e-bay, I understand how he feels. I also remember this adorable little boy who had his picture taken with Grant after he signed his red football on the day before the Super Bowl. How cute, I thought. Then I saw the football and picture on e-bay, and I was furious. I wondered if the little kid had been rented out to go to sporting events to get autographs only to sell them on e-bay. I hope the little boy got a fair cut!

As I look at the man Grant has become, I am extremely proud of him. At 25, he appears to have a handle on his fame and fortune. There are still differences I would like to see in his life, but we all feel that way about our children. I want him to be perfect, but he is still just 25 years old with goals, dreams, and problems.

I have become better about hearing criticism that is aimed at Grant. I, also realize that he can't make everyone happy, and no matter what he does there will always be some football he didn't sign or some quote he didn't say. There will always be someone waiting for him to fail so they can say "I told you so." After winning the Super Bowl, there was a huge parade in St. Louis. It was televised and the entire nation could see Grant celebrating. After several people made comments to me about his "behavior", I mentioned it to Chance. As always Chance put it all in perspective.

"Mom," he said, "what did he actually do that was wrong? Did he say anything bad? Did he hit anyone? Was he on drugs? There was probably more celebrating after Webb City won the football championship. And what do you think all these people commenting about Grant would be doing if they were 21 and just won a Super Bowl? Anyway, what did he do that was wrong? He's a good kid. He's good to everyone, including you, so what major sin did he commit? Lighten up. Just be happy for him." Out of the mouths of babes!

I know that Grant is a role model. Personally, I think he's a good one. But, he's like most men I know. He's just a little boy in a big body. He just has more toys!

In The End

I always tell people if Grant had been our first child, he might have been an only child. But you can see we didn't stop with Grant. After having Grant, I would have liked to have had a girl, but I just knew I'd have a basketball team. When Tracey came, I remembered what that nurse had said about boys.

Tracey was like Chance. He was an extremely good baby, or maybe Ron and I were just too busy or too tired to notice. Like all younger children, Tracey was always being dragged around. We didn't worry if he was on schedule or if he had on clean clothes. We knew if he kissed the dog, he wouldn't die, or if he ate dessert before dinner, he'd still like vegetables. The boys always say we were easier on Trace, but I think it's because we weren't as worried about being the perfect parents or having the perfect child. The funny thing is Tracey is our perfectionist. He's our thinker, our planner. He's been a delightful middle-age challenge. He's been the perfect end to for our family.

Looking back at Tracey as a baby, what I remember the most is enjoying him. With Chance, we were worried that we had to do everything according to the books. We worried about following rules, doing the right thing. With Grant, we just worried if he'd sleep that night or eat without throwing up. By the time Tracey arrived, we were older and wiser, and I can remember really enjoying rocking and cuddling Tracey. Since he was the last one, I appreciated everything I did with him. The sad part is that Ron and I were also so involved with Grant and Chance that Trace often did just get thrown in the car seat for another trip to a ballgame.

Tracey always sucked his thumb and carried his "blankie." To this day he still says that he suffered psychological problems as a result of my "losing" his blankie. He looked so cute with his big eyes and his tiny thumb up to his face. The blankie and thumb were probably his way of handling all the confusion and mayhem that went on in our house. From the time Trace was little, he always had to compete with the big boys, and no one gave him any slack. Ron has always said that Tracey has the most raw talent, and I'm sure it's a result of constantly playing with older kids.

Although he's the youngest, Trace always wanted to do what his brothers were doing. When we moved to Florida, we had a pool. The rule was that Trace couldn't even walk out by with pool without his life jacket. He showed no fear of water as he would run full speed into the pool. In T-ball he played shortstop, but the coach had to tell him to stay in one place because

Tracey fishing in the Keys

when the other kids couldn't catch the ball, he'd cover their positions. He started playing football in second grade, he easily learned the rules, and he became impatient when coaches had to slow the game down because most little second graders aren't capable of comprehending high school plays.

Of the three, Trace is the most competitive. Ron would encourage this by always making everything a contest. It used to drive me crazy, but whatever they did, the boys were always in competition with each other and their dad. I always joke that the boys would bet on who could spend the most money in the shortest time, but that's really how they approach things. I don't think we ever had a friendly game of anything. Now, I don't agree with this, but it may have helped the boys achieve the success they've achieved. It's hard to believe, but Grant was the least competitive of the boys. He'd get bored with a game and want to quit, and the boys would argue he couldn't quit until they would have a chance to win. Grant never really cared about winning unless it was something important with something on the line, like a football game. I think that explains why Grant doesn't always practice as hard as Ron thinks he should, but during a game he always comes through. Now when the boys get together, they still wrestle or shoot baskets, etc. to see who's the best, and Tracey is usually the one who wants to continue the competition until he wins.

Trace didn't always seem concerned about making us happy, but he never wanted anyone to be upset with him. It was just too much of a hassle to have someone upset. Tracey wants to do the right thing because it's easier to do the right thing. I think that Tracey spent a lot of time sucking his thumb and observing Chance and Grant. He knew what happened to them when they got into trouble, and he decided at an early age it just wasn't' worth the trouble. Having Dad upset or getting grounded wasn't how he intended to spend his time.

In school it is the same way. Tracey has learned that doing what you are supposed to do is a lot easier than bucking the system. I'm sure he drives some teachers crazy because he is the type of student who wants to know exactly what is expected of him. He wants to be assured he's doing things the "right" way. At times, Tracey drives me crazy because we are different personalities. I don't worry about detail, and Trace is a detail person. If it takes time to do it right, then he takes the time. When he was four and we started going to the Keys, he would sit for hours fishing. He would be the first one up in the morning and the last one to bed at night. He would talk to other fishermen about what they were using. He listened and learned. He's like that in sports. He seems to soak up what is going on around him.

As Tracey grew, he was a quieter child than either Chance or Grant. Everything was always "fine" or "OK." The only way I usually found out what was going on his life was to talk to his friends. They would tell everything. Tracey believes in the "need to know" policy, and unfortunately he didn't often think we had a need to know.

In the same respect Tracey did a lot of great things that we never heard about unless someone else told us. Sometimes I feel

Tracey playing hurt for Webb City Cardinals

that Trace kept quiet because he didn't want to be compared to Chance or Grant. Although Ron and I never felt that we did any comparing, I'm sure Trace was aware that others were always lumping the three boys together. It's only been lately that Trace has really seemed to open up to us. I think he finally feels that he is his own person. He's made a name for himself as Tracey Wistrom, not Chance or Grant Wistrom's little brother.

There will always be people who think Trace is at Nebraska because of Grant, but I'm sure that Nebraska head coach Frank Solich will tell you that there isn't a college anywhere that will offer a scholarship to a player just because of his brother. Looking back I'm sure Tracey is glad he chose Nebraska. He's happy with his life. He's looking forward to finishing his career and becoming a math teacher and a coach. Things couldn't have turned out any better for him!

Today I love being around Trace. He has the funniest sense of humor. My biggest problem with Tracey is he is so cotton pickin' honest. Once I was talking to Tracey about how I often felt his dad should have helped me more around the house or been more concerned about my problems. I really expected Trace to agree with me, but he looked at me, shook his head, and said, " Let me see, Mom. You've wrecked 12 cars, almost got Dad thrown in jail because he told you to pay off a car loan and you spent the money, and your credit cards were so high your son had to get an NFL contract to pay them off. Frankly Mom, I don't think you've had it too tough. If I had been Dad I would have probably left you after you wrecked the Corvette!"

Tracey sees things in black and white with little gray area. He's very practical and down to earth. When he was 16, and we discussed the fact that if he didn't want to rebuild a car he would have to drive the Mazda. His response was, "So what? People shouldn't just like you for your car anyway."

In addition to being very practical, Tracey is also very thoughtful. Last year for my birthday he made a CD of my favorite songs. One of the songs is about how "Daddies teach us how to catch and throw," but when things get tough it's a mama's love that little boys need. That was the year Grant rented a limo and sent Ron and me to a Tina Turner concert. Of course the boys gave Trace a lot of trash about how much I loved the hokey CD which hadn't cost near as much as their gifts. Tracey just sat there and grinned!

Even today, when we all get together, Tracey still asks if I listen to the song? I tell him "yes" and remind him not to forget that little boys always need their mother's love.

In The Future

Often I remember what that nurse said when Grant was born. Whatever God's reason, I'm thrilled that he saw three boys as a part of his plan for me. As each one of the boys has walked off the football field in their sweaty uniforms to hug me, I've often asked myself how I could have been so lucky. What was I thinking, wishing for a girl?

And what could make this picture complete? Maybe little grandbabies, boys or girls; this time I won't question the Big Guy in the Sky!

Grant, Tracey, Chance in Florida

A
ABILITY AND ATTITUDE

Everyone always thought our three boys were blessed with an unbelievable ability to play ball - any kind of ball! The truth is they were all just normal little guys with normal playing ability. What they were blessed with is a father who taught them to take their ability and mix it with practice and patience and a "never say die attitude."

Ron's theory was that in order to be successful in anything-football or whatever - you had to give 100 percent. Now, I honestly never quite understood how you could give 100 percent, but somehow he made the boys believe that THEY could, and that's what often gave them the edge.

Oh sure, you're saying, no ability? OK, they were always big for their age, but so are a lot of boys who didn't get college scholarships. So while size certainly played a role in their achievements, they honestly had to work for everything they earned. Ron taught them that you never quit. If you fail, you pick yourself up and start again. Chance had a coach in Florida who told him that he would never start in a varsity game. One father told Ron when Grant was a freshman that it was a shame Grant was so uncoordinated as all the other players would probably pass him up. Tracey always had players from opposing teams make comments like, "You're never be as good as your brother!" If the boys had listened to what others said, they would have never played college ball. However, they developed an attitude that prevented them from quitting. Now that they've all been named All-Americans, I think they've proven my point.

From the time they were little, we praised their abilities, no matter how big or small they were, and Ron showed them where they needed to improve. When he played ball with them, he never let them win or gave them a break because he was "bigger." Ron and I often disagreed on this strategy. I'd give the boys hints in Pictionary or I'd slow down at the end of the race, but not Ron. He'd go one-on-one with them as if they were adults. And surprisingly enough, they loved it. They knew when they beat Dad, they had won fair and square. And he was the first one to praise them for it. Even today Grant and Trace will always look to see if Dad is smiling after the game because then they know they have done well.

Unlike some fathers who constantly tell their kids what great athletes they are, Ron usually downplayed the boys' performances. He never told them "they were the best" or "the coach doesn't know anything." Instead he'd be the first to say what they did wrong, another point I often disagreed with.

Grant loves to tell about the time that his dad was going to make him walk home after a game because he hadn't played as well as Ron thought he should have played. I don't actually remember it happening quite that way, but it makes a great story, and it shows how Ron always expected the boys to use what ability they had and make the most of it. Ability?

I'm sure 75 percent of starting freshmen football players have the ability to play college ball, but it's the attitude about that ability that projects success. It's an attitude that has to start in backyard baseball. It's an attitude that says, "I may not be the best at what I do, but I'll do the best with what I have. It doesn't matter how good I think I am or how good my dad thinks I am, it's what I DO that counts." Talk is cheap!

Yes, there are some kids who seem to have a natural ability, but I bet if you could go back to their childhood days, you'd see that they were always playing ball of some kind. They're the kids who went to early weights and didn't quit when the coach yelled at them. In gym class they hustled because as athletes they knew it was expected of them. They're also the kids that coaches push a little more because coaches recognize their potential.

Parents, if your child tells you that "the coach is always picking on me," or the coach is always telling your son that he can run a little faster, you should thank the coach. He's probably "picking on him" because, as the Army says, the coach wants your son to be all that he can be! Believe me, I used to think that their high school coaches, Coach Thompson and Coach Wall, were tougher on my boys, but I soon learned that it was because they knew what the boys were capable of doing.

They also knew that the boys had a father who would never be upset over anything that the coaches had done or said to the boys! My personal opinion is that coaches either ignore or manage to get rid of players who don't produce. They push the play makers. So, maybe the next time you watch practice you'll be glad when the coach yells at your child.

Can you imagine the look on a coach's face if a parent were to walk up to him and say, "I wish you'd make my boy work harder, run a little faster. You're just not being tough enough on him!"

If your child truly wants to be successful in sports, he or she needs to develop an attitude that accepts criticism and learns from it. Instead of whining or complaining about a coach, the player needs to keep his mouth shut and listen and learn. At least if he doesn't play beyond high school, what he learns on the field will prepare him for life. The attitude a player develops concerning teamwork, work ethics, time management, setting goals, and other skills learned in sports will teach him more about responsibility than anything a parent or even a teacher can say.

B
BELIEVE

As a teacher and a mother, I know the most important concept a child can learn is to believe in himself. If I can convince a child that he or she can make an A in English, at least that child will try. Some children refuse to try because they have been told over and over that they can't do it; they can't succeed. It doesn't matter how smart a child is, or how well he can play sports, because if he doesn't believe he can be successful, then he won't. If he doesn't believe he can make the throw from home to second or throw a touchdown pass, he won't be able to do it. There's a big difference in an obnoxious spoiled brat who thinks he's the best player on the team because his dad said so and an unassuming child who believes in himself because he's developed his ability through practice.

If a parent constantly belittles a child in front of his peers, the child will begin to feel he is a stupid, lousy football player. And if a parent constantly tells a child he's the best player on the team and the coach is too stupid to know it, then the child believes that also. I've seen both kinds of students in my class, and it's a crime what their parents have done to them.

In the first case, where the child is constantly told how stupid he is, the child will tell you how stupid he is and so what's the point of trying? Usually these parents have been unsuccessful, so they berate their children because it makes them feel better. Those kids are afraid to try and why should they practice? The people who they love the most are telling them they'll never amount to anything anyway. And guess what, they usually do fail. So they don't play well, and their parents yell at them again, "So why can't you play like that Smith kid?"

Eventually the little guy throws his glove down, and says, "I quit! You like this stinkin' game so much, you play it!" I actually witnessed this one summer.

Don't get me wrong, Ron would occasionally yell, "Use your head!" And once again I would want to punch him in the mouth. But Ron wasn't the kind of father who criticized his boys from the recliner. He'd go out and show them what they were doing wrong and how to correct it. He made them believe they could do it by showing them that hard work and patience would help them achieve their goals. Ron was realistic about the boys' abilities.

In fact, I always thought that he was too realistic. When Ron was coaching the boys, I always wanted him to have the boys play

quarterback or pitcher. Let's face it, they get the glory. Ron always explained that those weren't the positions they were best suited to play. My response was that he was the coach and he could put his players anywhere he wanted! Of course you know who won that argument as I have no quarterbacks. Tracey did play quarterback until he got hurt his freshman year. When he came back he had been replaced with a young man who was doing a great job. I was very disappointed, but Tracey learned that those things happen. When

Tracey at Nebraska

they do than you have to shake the dust off your cleats and find another position. You can't quit or pout or feel sorry for yourself. It's just like the song says, "You've got to have high hopes!"

However, I do have to admit that every time I watch Peyton Manning, I think that Tracey would have made an awesome quarterback. But he's pretty happy doing what's he's doing, and that's what we really want for our children.

So, if you're a screamer who feels that your son could never play in the NFL, he probably never will. If you don't believe in your child, than who will?

On the other hand, there are parents who always blame everyone else for what their kids do wrong. "The teacher doesn't like him. The coach has always had it in for him. Life just hasn't been fair to my kids."

They're right; life isn't fair. That's why kids have to be taught to go that extra mile to be successful. They have to BELIEVE they can do it, but they have to be willing to work.

Whenever the boys tried to tell me they got a bad grade because the teacher didn't like them, I'd laugh and say, "Oh honey, you're so sweet and cute, I can't believe someone wouldn't find you adorable." So that theory didn't work in our household.

You can't teach kids to believe in themselves by blaming everyone else. There are too many adults today who blame the world for their problems. There's a fine line in believing you can do it and doing it, or just talking about it and blaming someone else for why you didn't do it.

All parents want their children to be successful, noticed, and admired; but, the training has to begin at home. Often when children don't make the team, we, as parents, are embarrassed because it reflects on us. Rather than admit we may have failed as parents, it's easier to blame someone else. And too often that's the easy way out.

In Peter Pan, he tells the audience that they have to believe in order to save Tinkerbell. Sometimes we have to become Peter Pan.

C
COACHES

The first coach who ever criticized the boys was Ron. He was their head coach in both youth baseball and football. Ron laid the groundwork for how he expected his boys to respond to future coaches. And the boys will quickly agree that Ron was the hardest coach that they ever had! They will also tell you that playing for Big R was the best preparation they could have had for the future.

I always thought that Ron was harder on our boys, and maybe he was; but, whatever it was, it worked! As far as coaching the other players, they loved Ron. Ron was tough, but he was honest and fair. Even today we still get letters from parents who have seen Grant or Trace on TV, so they know where we're living. They'll

Chance, Grant, Coach Wall, Tracey

write and tell Ron how much he helped their boys, not just with football but life. If you're thinking about being a youth coach, make sure you're doing it for the right reasons. If you're doing it so that you can make your child a super star, then maybe you should sit this year out.

What about our other experiences with other coaches? Like everyone else in sports, our boys have had good coaches, great coaches, mean coaches, fair coaches, all kinds. I could go on and on considering how many coaches our boys have had. They've had some great coaches like Coach Thompson and Coach Wall who were their high school coaches. Chance said he thought Coach Correll was one of the few men who knew more about football than Ron, and you can't do much better than the college coaches the boys played under. And they've had terrible coaches like - nope, as much as I'd like to, I won't go there.

And yes, all three boys had some rotten coaches; coaches who didn't keep their promises, coaches who played their sons instead of the better players, coaches who played favorites. Chance had a coach in Pop Warner football who would never let him play although every child at that level is supposed to get in the game, and Chance was the better player. But Chance was the new kid on the block and the coach had already decided on his team. Ha, you're saying! The woman is just like another mother who thinks her kid is better than any other. (We mothers do stick together.) The difference is I had now lived with Ron Wistrom for 10 years, and he was and always is the first to say whether our boys should be playing or not. And when he told me Chance should be in the game, I did get extremely upset with the coach. But no, we didn't complain to the coach. That's a Cardinal sin at the Wistrom house.

I can still remember watching that hot, sweaty, little boy follow the coach up and down the field afraid to take his helmet off for fear the coach would put him in the game and he'd miss his chance if he couldn't get his helmet fastened in time. This went on for about three games, and believe me I thought of unspeakable things I wanted to do to that man, but again we never complained about the coach in front of the boys. Our boys grew up with that attitude of respect for coaches, and I can't help but believe that respect paid off for them.

Today in my classes I try to tell my students to always be respectful. If it comes down to two players with the same ability the coach will choose the one who exhibits respect and consideration toward others.

Ron, Chance, Kathy after a CMSU game

Anyway, back to Chance. Yes, he should have played. He never missed practice; he did whatever he was told; and he WAS the better player. By the end of the third, game I was ready to tell him to quit. Wistrom rule # 2: You never quit what you start. You don't have to ever sign-up again, but you never, ever quit because you're not only letting yourself down, but you're letting your teammates down also. So quitting was out of the question. And Chance continued to practice and sit on the bench.

At this same time we were also trying to teach Chance about the value of money. Chance had been saving for a new bike that he had in lay-away. He was about $75 short, so one day after a painful and excruciating hot day on the bench for both of us, I loaded Chance in the truck and made a bee-line for Sears where his bike was.

Ron had to work that day, so when we pulled up in the driveway, Ron looked at the bike in the back as I glared at him and I said, "He didn't get to play today and that's that!" Not another word was said!

Ron had as difficult of a time that year as Chance did. He didn't always think the boys deserved to play over another player. He was always the first to say, "Yeah, I would have taken Grant out, too. He's not helping the team." But he believes in fairness. If a player is better at that position than that player should play despite who his dad is.

I can and do relate to children and parents who "ride the pine." But don't criticize the coach because that won't help your child. The good guy does win. It may take a while before you or your son realizes it, but eventually the hard work pays off.

I would love to go back to Florida and look that coach in the eye and tell him how Chance played college football at a major Missouri college, but I'm sure he wouldn't be impressed. He had his own personal agenda, and Chance wasn't a part of it. It was very hard on Chance's self-esteem, but constantly berating the coach wouldn't have helped. (I think the bike did!!)

Coaches really do have one of the toughest and most important jobs in the world. In some cases, coaches are father figures to young men who have never had any male role model to admire. Coaches become mentors, friends, the best man at weddings. What a coach says to a young man may influence that young man wherever he goes. As a teacher, it used to bug me that good coaches were in higher demand than good English teachers. However, since I've become so well acquainted with coaches I've changed my mind.

I know how important then Webb City High School football coach, Coach Kill was to Chance when we moved back to Missouri. I can still see Coach K's car sitting up at the high school from 6:00 a.m. to 10:00 p.m. Coach Kill made a group of young men believe they could win a state championship. Not having children of their own, Webb City coaches Thompson and Johnson seemed to adopt their players. Having a son who coaches, I know the concern and love he feels for his boys. So, whatever people may think of coaches, if you totaled the hours against the money, they probably don't make minimum wage! Then you factor in a community with a winning tradition, and the pressure is on. Coaching is not an easy job, as I once thought.

Another point I'd like to make is that coaches' wives have a lot of pressure on them. Considering all the time a coach spends on everyone else's children, it leaves very little time for his own family and wife. So before you call a coach at home, think about what I said. Coaches deserve time with their own families after all the time they've spent solving other children's problems. And this is another reason you shouldn't talk about the coach in the stands. No young woman should have to hear her husband being raked over the coals. I used to tell people that I was going to get a T-shirt that said, "Yes, I'm Coach Wistrom's wife and sometimes I think he's a jerk, but that doesn't mean you can say he is!"

As a mother of players and now coaches, I think I've seen both sides of the fence. Here are some rules I think both parents and coaches should follow:

RULES FOR PARENTS
1. Let the coach, coach. Don't complain to him.
2. Don't complain about the coach in front of your children.
3. Don't blame the coach for your son's ability. Maybe there really is another player better than your son.
4. Ask your son, instead of the coach, why he isn't playing. He probably knows.
5. If your son has a problem, tell him to talk to the coach, not you.
6. Don't pressure the coach with threats about "who you know."
7. Make sure you hear both sides of the story before you start complaining (Good advice for parents and teachers, also!)
8. Don't confront a coach in front of others.
9. Don't call a coach at home.
10. Don't compare coaches or styles.
11. Don't get upset or even listen to what is said or done at practice.
12. Make sure your kids are on time for practices and games, and pick them up on time.
13. If your child has to miss practice (even if he's sick) than be prepared for the idea that he will probably spend some time on the bench. If that's the rule, then it's a rule.

14. Don't discuss the coach or the players in the stands. You never know whose wife or mother is sitting there. (I always wear a jersey that says Wistrom. If someone is dumb enough to comment about one of MY babies, than they'd better be prepared to hear what I have to say.)
15. Don't compare last year's team to this year's team. All players are different.
16. Attend all parents' meetings. Be supportive.

I really do know how tough it is to keep your mouth shut when you don't think your child is getting a fair shake, but I do know that complaining about it won't (or shouldn't) help. Try to get your son to talk privately with the coach about why he isn't playing more. Talk to him about how to talk to the coach. Make sure he looks the coach in the eye and forces the coach to give him reasons, not excuses. If that really doesn't work, then make an appointment to speak to the coach privately. Don't walk in with a chip on your shoulder. Be rational, discuss your feelings calmly and be prepared for the answer. Don't walk in with the idea that you know where and when your child should play. Remember you're asking why your son isn't playing, not telling the coach that your son should be playing. If you have a personal agenda for the coach, you're probably going to be disappointed when you leave.

Tracey and Kathy after a Webb City game

I truly believe that coaches go into coaching because they love working with kids. Most coaches really do want both kids and parents to be happy, and why wouldn't they. Honestly, a coach is not out to "get your child" or make your life miserable. They want to build character, and yes, they want to win. Their jobs depend on it!

RULES FOR COACHES

1. Be honest and fair. If you have a rule that after being late three times, a player doesn't get to start, then enforce it. Don't just enforce it for the second team players.
2. Don't just tell players what they want to hear. If a player isn't going to get much playing time, than tell them and tell them why. Maybe they can get better.
3. Don't "put down" other coaches or sports. Don't make kids choose between sports. In high school kids should be able to play what they want. I do think if a child has a chance for a college scholarship than he should be encouraged to work more at that sport. Be honest about it.
4. If the score gets ridiculously high, then let everyone play. And let them play longer than 25 seconds.
5. Remember it's the kids who play the game, not an over-bearing, influential parent. I know this can be difficult because it's often "the squeaky wheel that gets oiled." If all possible, don't let loud, obnoxious parents influence you. My boys can tell you which mamas complained the loudest, and the sad thing is it seemed to work. My only consolation, since I wasn't allowed to question coaches, is that once these young players get to college, the best player (not the loudest parent) plays.
6. Make everyone follow the same rules. Don't have separate rules for the super stars and another set of rules for the third team. All players can tell you exactly who broke what rule and why it was ignored. They know which parents complain and what's done about it. What's good for the goose should be good for the gander. Believe me, everyone knows exactly what's going on, especially in a small town! I know I really harp on this issue through out this book, but I truly believe this is one

of the biggest problems with the youth of today. We tell students to follow the rules, work hard, be honest, yada, yada, yada, and we adults don't do it!

7. Remember that these really are little boys with feelings and hopes and dreams. You, as a coach, probably have more influence over them than their parents. It's a big job with a lot of responsibility.

Here's where I'm supposed to say that "winning isn't everything;" however, having been around a long time, I know that winning is what pays the bills. I just hope that it's never at the cost of a young man. I must admit Ron and I weren't overly thrilled when Chance announced he was going to change professions. Teaching has changed and so has coaching. There's more pressure on everyone in education. But, I also know that our country needs more role models for kids, especially in the teaching profession.

Whether you agree or not, sports will always be important in our society, especially when you pay a basketball player more than you pay the President. If your community is fortunate enough to have good coaches who lead by example, even if they don't win every game, then you should try to keep them. Don't let a disgruntled parent interfere. If you have young men and women who are trying to instill values in young people, then support them, encourage them.

On the other hand, if you have coaches who say "win at all costs, ignore the rules," then I'd say you have a problem. It's a tough line to walk, and I admire anyone who takes the challenge.

D

DETERMINATION & DEDICATION

Determination goes right along with attitude, ability, and believing. If I knew how to teach children to have determination, I'd write a book about that; however, I do know that Ron did it with our boys. He incorporated it with everything he taught the boys. It comes into play when you teach kids to never quit.

I'm not sure when they "learned" it, but I can tell you the experiences that come to mind when I think of the word.

Chance - When we moved to Florida in 1981, Chance contacted bacterial meningitis two days before we were scheduled to leave. He had to stay behind with his grandparents, Gammy and Grandpa. He had to stay quiet in a dark room. And for entertainment, Gammy and Grandpa played cards with him while he dined on homemade ice cream and chocolate pie from his Aunt Claudia. When he was finally able to come to Florida he looked more like Shamu when he got off the plane!

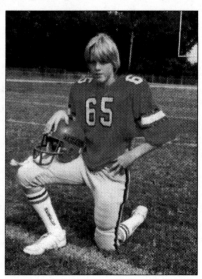

Naturally he was upset about leaving his home, but he was excited about playing football in Florida. He had heard about the teams and bowl games, and he was ready to play. The problem

Chance after losing 20lbs in Florida

was, he was going into the fifth grade, but his body looked like he should be on the junior varsity! Florida has weight requirements instead of age, and, because of his weight, he would have had to play with ninth graders. Now size is one thing, but there's a BIG difference between the mentality of a fifth grader and that of a ninth grader. In order to play with his own age group he had to lose 20 pounds in six weeks. Well, I can tell you that short of cutting off both of my legs, there's no way I could loose that kind of weight in six months!

So, I tried to steer Chance to soccer or band or anything that didn't have a weight limit! But, in our family, it was and still is FOOTBALL! So Ron developed a weight training program for Chance.

Now Ron wouldn't let Chance do anything stupid like sit in the attic wearing trash bags (and I do know some young wrestlers who did that!), but, he did give Chance a daily exercise program. Bobby Bowden could have used it. Chance would run several times a day, do laps in the pool, and watch his diet. I felt so sorry for him that I tried to run with him, but I couldn't do it. I'm embarrassed to say that I'd poop out about the second block, so I'd sit and wait for him. He would round the corner with red, puffy cheeks and teary eyes. Then we would sit and cry together. I would tell him to quit; football wasn't THAT important. Dad wouldn't care. I even offered to just tell Dad we ran; it would be our secret. But even at that age, Chance loved and respected his dad so much that he wouldn't deceive him. He kept running and swimming and eating his veggies, and he lost the 20 pounds. I personally believe that my first-born son is capable of doing anything he sets his mind to, and I think he feels that way also.

Maybe he would have turned out that way without this lesson in self-control, maybe not. I only know that chubby little boy had more grit and determination than his 33-year old mother. That victory in determination and dedication gave Chance a heart that never says die, and that's something you can't learn from a book! It came in handy when his high school freshman football coach (who was really a soccer coach) told him he'd never play college ball, much less varsity!

It surfaced again when he graduated with a degree in industrial hygiene and then decided he really wanted to teach and coach although it would take him another two years to get his degree. And now that he's working with young people, he can honestly talk to them about determination and work ethics - been there and done that! People who put-down sports have no idea of life's lessons that are learned on the field!

Grant - Everyone, including his mother, always thought that things were easier for Grant. He always seemed to be at the right place at the right time. Grant never talks about his work; he just does it. It wasn't until I read his and Jason Peter's book, *Heart and Soul*, that I realized how dedicated he was and is, and how hard he works at being the best he can be. In the book he discusses how determined they were to prove Nebraska was the Number One team; how he and Jason felt they had to show the younger players how to develop a winning attitude through hard work and dedication. It would have been easy for them to sit back and be happy with the adoration that they were shown as seniors at Nebraska, but they didn't. Instead it's been said that they worked twice as hard as anyone else did during the summer.

Grant has had to prove himself all over again as an NFL player. It devastates me, as his mother, to read some of the material I've seen written about Grant as a Ram. Remember, I spent four years reading things about Grant at Nebraska that would make a mother's heart swell with pride. We still hear from people who think Grant should run for election in Nebraska; we still get special treatment at restaurants! It really breaks my heart to believe that adults could have hollered obscenities at this 21-year old before he even had a chance to prove what he could do; however, when I mentioned my feelings to Grant, once again my heart swelled with pride as he explained he understood why people were frustrated, and yes, he'd have to prove himself all over again!

He's very adult about it, and he's working as hard as he can to make St.Louis fans believe in him. It would have been easy for him to believe all those wonderful things said about him in Nebraska,

Grant and Tracey in the Keys

but then he would have to believe what some were saying about him in the NFL. Instead Grant knows what he has to do, and he is determined to do it just like he and Jason said in *Heart and Soul*. If he had been raised to believe he could be "great" just because he's Grant, then he woul not be where he is today. He knows about determination and dedication. I'm not sure when he learned it, but he did. He was taught that you never quit or give up, and you certainly don't rely on what you did yesterday.

Tracey- Depending how you look at it, Tracey either had it really, really good or really, really bad being Chance's and Grant's little brother. It may have opened doors for him, but once he got in, everyone expected the same of him. Ron has always said that Tracey has more raw talent than either Grant or Chance. But Tracey also wants to be the best at whatever he does. He is more competitive than the others, and sports obviously were and are a big part of his life. People watched and expected Tracey to be good, and he was. But he has also worked as hard as anyone has on the team. He has always had to prove that he's where he is today because of what he does, not who he is.

In his freshman year of high school he dislocated his knee during an early fall practice. Grant was there, and he says it was completely twisted around to the back. It was fortunate that he didn't need surgery as that could have ended his football days, but the rebuilding period required him to do painful exercises with patience and grit. Again, I would have said, "That's all, folks!" But I don't think the thought ever entered his mind. Instead he followed the vigorous training and he was back sooner than expected. He was determined to play again and play well!

When Tracey first got hurt, I discussed the fact that he might not be able to play football again. I could tell that most people were thinking, "Good Lord, woman, it's only a game. It could be so much worse." Of course, I know that. I am reminded everyday that are so many things that happen far more devastating than a career-ending injury. But if you have a child who loves sports, you know what I'm talking about!

Watching the films of the state basketball playoffs, you can see that determination in his eyes. His class had lost its chance for a football title, and you could see it in his face that he wasn't going to lose another opportunity to win a championship. Actually the entire team displayed that never-say-die attitude. It was like a magic moment because the boys never quit. They willed themselves to win!

At Nebraska, Tracey had to prove himself. The big discussion was whether Tracey was big enough to play the tight end position for the Huskers. I had no doubt after living with the boy for 20 years that through determination and hard work he WOULD earn a starting position.

Along with determination, children must also be dedicated, but dedication is a family thing. When we decided to be parents, Ron and I dedicated our lives to being the best parents we could be. I don't think it was a conscious decision, but as each boy came along, we realized how raising children is a job that requires work. We also decided that they would be the most important job we would ever have.

I used the traditional mother's approach. I'd love them, correct them, and reward them. I'd do all the things a mom does. But, I honestly believe that Ron understood parenthood better than I did. (I really hate to admit that!) When the boys decided to do anything, Ron took an active part in it. And we dedicated our lives to those things. If Ron expected the boys to give 110 percent to a baseball team, then we, as parents, had to give 110 percent. If we expected them to be responsible about practices, then we had to be. You can't blame kids when they're late to practice because their parents were late driving them. I know problems arise, but why should a child accept responsibility when his parents don't? And usually these are the parents who complain that no one gives their kids a chance. Coaches are only human, and they do get upset when kids are late to practice or parents are late picking them up.

We used to go places on spring break, but then it interfered with baseball. We haven't been together as a family on Christmas since Grant went to Nebraska. One time we had a trip planned and Chance had all-star practice, so we left him with the family of another player on the team. It sounds terrible, but Chance knew he was expected to be at practice, like everyone else. We knew if he wasn't there than the team couldn't practice as a team.

I agree that family time is more important that a baseball game, but I also believe that as children get older they have to make dif-

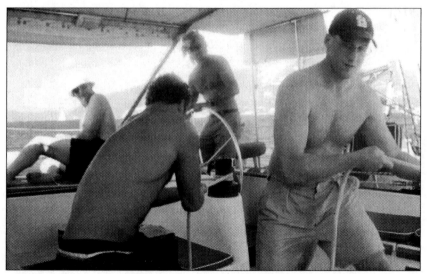

All the boys work together on a cruise

ficult decisions and choices. Now I'm not talking about nine- and ten-year olds. Personally I don't think they should be travelling all over the country to play in all star games. I'm talking about older kids. If your child commits to a team, then he needs to put that team as his first priority. If he wants to go on vacation, then he should be prepared for someone taking his position. There are plenty of little guys, like my sons, who are willing to give up a vacation for a chance to play.

Parents if your child chooses the trip to Florida over hot practices (and I can't say I blame him) than both you and he should be prepared to see him sit on the bench when you return. It's a matter of priorities. In our family, team commitment was the top priority. Coaches, if you make the rule about missing practices or games, then you, too, should be prepared to make your best player sit the bench. That used to really tick me off. Our kids were always at practices, but there were times that a better player would miss, and he'd go right back to the position he had.

We never thought that our boys were good enough that they could afford to miss practices or games, so we never did. They didn't want to take a chance of losing their positions. I know there were times that other parents may have thought our boys got "special" treatment, but if they did it was because they were dedicated. They were on time, they didn't miss practices or games, and they followed the rules. So did we! We always had family time, but it usually revolved around sporting events. Our social life was the baseball park or the football stadium. Looking back, I wouldn't have missed it for the world!

I've logged more time at football games than most referees have! Up until this year, Ron hadn't missed but one of any of the boys' high school or college games! This year we haven't been able to see all of Grant's games because we felt our first responsibility was to Tracey. If possible we try to see some of Chance's games.

The point is when the boys made a commitment we signed up at the same time. If they were in something, sports or whatever, we were there to watch. There were nights we'd leave after watching Tracey play Friday night football and drive six hours to see Grant play in Lincoln. Now we'll try to see some of Chance's games, drive to Lincoln and watch Trace, and then drive to St.Louis to watch Grant. Ron says his favorite times were watching Trace play junior high on Thursday, Grant play on Friday, and Chance play on Saturday.

Needless to say, I am both amazed and somewhat annoyed at parents who say they're just too tired or too busy to go to a game. I guarantee we could have found excuses, but there aren't any when your son is playing his heart out and Mom and Dad are eating dinner out because they know they have a free baby-sitter for a few hours while their children play baseball.

I have no patience for parents like that, and they have no right to complain about or criticize either their children or the coach. Again there are circumstances that make things more difficult, but we juggled jobs and three boys who played in everything. Ron had to travel a lot, but our top priority was and is, even today, the boys. We all like to be praised, and let's face it; kids, like adults, do better and work harder when they know someone is watching them. It breaks my heart too see some little guy waiting around for someone to pick him up after a game.

Whatever it takes, if you have children participating in something, you need to be there. When the boys played soccer, and Ron REALLY dislikes soccer, we were there. Once we sat for two hours in a hot, metal building to watch Grant wrestle. By the time we stood up and clapped and sat down, he had been pinned!

We never missed the parents' meetings for football. Although by the time we had attended the third one we knew what the coach would say before he said it. The coaches knew we appreciated what they did, and we, as a family, were dedicated to their goals. Good coaches work extremely hard to develop character and goals in young children, and we should be willing to give them as much time as they are willing to give our children.

Coaches are dedicated.

Children are dedicated.

And we, as parents, must also be dedicated. The game you miss may be the one where your son scores the winning touchdown, and I can think of nothing that could possibly be more important than that.

Absolutely NOTHING!

E, F, G
EXCUSES, FAILURE, GRANDPARENTS

I lumped these three together because the only poeple who should accept excuses for failure are grandparents.

Our boys have failed at things, but they weren't allowed to make excuses for their behavior. Instead they were expected to learn from their mistakes. They had to accept the part they played in their own failure. Maybe they looked slow on the football field because they had stayed up too late. If they were taken out of the game, then it wasn't the coach's fault, it was their fault. Perhaps they needed to watch the Tom Emanski batting tape *ONE MORE TIME* to improve their hitting. If the boys weren't doing well, Ron told them they couldn't blame anyone but themselves.

Grandpa and Gammy in the Keys

When Grant was a senior he had straight As in school. Now, this really wasn't that difficult for Grant, as he is smart and he can easily learn and retain information. Like all the boys, he made good grades. And it may sound terrible, but we didn't accept C's. As a teacher, I knew what the boys were capable of doing, and they were capable of A's. This doesn't mean that we wouldn't have accepted C's if that's all they could do. It just means that we expected them to work up to their full potential.

Anyway, back to Grant. He made a C in his English class. I knew he had a very demanding teacher, but I also knew she was crazy about Grant. So, what happened, I asked? He told me that he had to leave early for a baseball game, and he hadn't turned in an assignment. The mother in me immediately assumed that she was probably ticked off because I knew she resented all the time spent on athletics. I went on and on about how teachers needed to remember that students had other school responsibilities, and since he was absent because of a school event then she should allow him to make-up the assignment.

Then after shooting off my mouth I found out that her policy was, and always had been, that anytime students were going to be gone for a school activity, then the students had to give her their work BEFORE they left for the activity. Grant had finished it, but he just forgot to turn it in before he left. Frankly, as a teacher, I probably would have accepted the late paper. Grant's a good kid, and she liked him. He thought she was one of the best teachers, although one of the toughest, who he ever had; however, she didn't accept it. And Grant accepted the C, and he accepted the hassle he got from his dad. He didn't try to blame her or make excuses.

I think Grant learned a valuable lesson about teachers, people, and life. He couldn't count on his charm to bail him out when he messed-up, he had to accept the responsibility for the C, and rules were rules. When we break them there are consequences. We have to decide if it's worth the consequence to break the rule.

Today too many parents try to bale their kids out of a bad situation. The parents make excuses for what their children do wrong, and no one wants to accept the consequences. I am amazed when kids destroy property and their parents don't think they should be responsible for the damages. Frankly I was embarrassed about the C, in English, of all things since I'm an English teacher. But, that's part of the problem. We are embarrassed when our kids mess-up because it reflects on us, the parents, which is why we try to bale our kids out.

I did make excuses for the boys. If they didn't have their homework finished, I'd blame it on football practice. When they didn't play as well as they should, it was because they'd been up late to do their homework. On the other hand, Big R didn't. He always had the boys discuss their mistakes and what caused them and how to prevent them from happening again. But he didn't allow them to make excuses.

As the boys grew older, they began to point out their own mistakes. After a game, they are the first to tell Dad what they did wrong and how they intend to correct it. I still say, "Oh, honey, you had a great game. I think your leg is still bothering you, though." And they smile and hug me and give Ron a knowing glance and say "Thanks, Mom."

On the other side, Grandmas always have excuses for their behavior. When Chance was little he would throw himself down spread-eagle in the middle of the grocery aisle demanding candy; however, according to Gammy, he wasn't being obnoxious, he was "displaying his independence."

Once Grant bit someone at the doctor's office. Gammy had come with me to help with the boys while they got their shots, and as he was throwing a tantrum. Gammy said to everyone who was

Grandpa and Gammy (standing) with Kathy (left), and Ron (right)
on Tracey's (center) signing day.

watching that "No wonder the poor baby is misbehaving; he does-n't feel well." Gammy wouldn't and still won't criticize them or allow anyone else to say anything about her precious little jewels.

At first, Ron and I had a difficult time dealing with the boys' behavior after they returned from Gammy and Grandpa's house; however, we finally reached an agreement. When the boys were at Gammy's it was like they were on a Disney vacation. They could eat what and when they wanted. They could do whatever they could talk Gammy into doing (and that covered a lot). It was like living at the Magic Kingdom. BUT, once they returned home, it was like going back to work. You had to do what the boss said, and in this case, we were the bosses. As long as they could "beam" themselves back to reality, they could behave however Gammy and Grandpa would let them. Occasionally, it was difficult to return to earth after being at Planet Grandma, but the travel rules were certainly worth the visits.

Now, that I am closer to being a grandma, I realize the value of grandparents everywhere. Ron and I were so lucky that his folks were close enough so the boys could see them whenever they wanted. I never understood parents who said, "Oh, I won't let him stay at Grandma's. I just couldn't bear to have him away from me." Or else they would complain about how spoiled their children would be when they returned. Or maybe they didn't like their in-laws so they would hurt them by keeping their children from knowing them.

Baloney!!! I always thought that we had many years to spend with the boys, and if the boys wanted to visit Gammy and GP, and they wanted the boys, I certainly didn't see a problem. When the boys were gone, Ron and I had time to be alone, and all marriages need that.

Looking back, those times the boys spent with Gammy and GP were probably some of the most special memories the boys have of growing-up. Wouldn't we all love to have a place where we can go and do no wrong; a place where we are brilliant and beautiful, funny and adorable? I don't know about you, but I'd love to have a place like that to visit where everyone thinks I am the best thing since peanut butter! And isn't that what childhood is supposed to be - a time when a little guy has no worries, no pressure, no problems except choosing what kind of ice cream he wants after dinner, or before!

It's sad to say, but there are too many little boys and girls who don't have the luxury of being spoiled by anyone. No one tells them how special they are or buys them toys they don't need. Unconditional love is a tricky thing, but grandmothers and grandfathers seem to have a handle on it.

If you're fortunate enough to have such parents, let your children be with them. Don't punish your children because you're mad at your parents. Children learn so much about love and compassion from grandparents, and grandparents, take advantage of spoiling them. They're only little for such a short time, take advantage of it. Everyone wins!! As my mother-in-law loves to say, "Well, being spoiled by Gammy certainly didn't hurt your boys. Just look how well they turned out. And if anyone says differently, they can just answer to me!"

Guess what? No one ever has!

H
HONESTY

I always feel that Ron is TOO honest with the boys. In fact I want him to sprinkle a few little white lies with his brutally honest analysis of their performances. But Ron's theory is that's what wrong with the world today: Nobody tells the truth. And you tell the truth, even if it hurts. In today's society we reward kids for just showing up at school, and now we want to pay them to go to summer school when the reason that they are going to summer school in the first place is because they didn't do anything during the year.

So, basically we're telling our kids that some employer is going to pay them just because they show up. I don't think so!

Ron's attitude is that sports activities prepare children for life; therefore, complete honestly is necessary for success. So, when the boys see us after a game, I hug and kiss them and tell them how great they were when I don't have a clue if they played a good game or not. I do know that Trace is supposed to score touchdowns when he catches the ball, but I never really understood what the other boys were supposed to do. (My sister, Dodie, is even worse than I am. She still calls Grant a "dead end", and Tracey is a "tailgate".)

On the other hand, Ron hugs them, and then they put their heads together and begin the post-game analysis. When the boys were little I hated the after-game huddles. If they got on the field, I was happy because that's my role as Mom. I like to stand around and bask in the glory! And Ron saw his role as the evaluator. He loves them and is just as proud of them as I am, if not more so because he actually understands their accomplishments. He just doesn't ever sugarcoat anything. He wanted them to be able to handle criticism, as well as critique themselves, not so much against other players but against their own performances.

Today all three of the boys are their own worst critics. Now Ron will start to say something about a certain play, and Trace will finish the analysis for him. The boys truly love and respect their dad for his unconditional love as well as his unconditional honesty.

And me? They love and respect me because I allow Ron to be the kind of father that he is. Allow probably isn't an accurate word. What I mean is Ron and I might have disagreed about how to raise the boys, but we never did it in front of them. I didn't always approve of how or why Ron said or did things, but I never criticized him in front of the boys. Plenty might have been said later, but I know how important it is for children, especially boys, to respect their father. Even if I was upset with Ron I would try and explain to the boys why he did or said what he did. Now that the boys are older, they attribute a lot their success to their dad. (Just check their interviews; at times you'd think they were in a single parent family!)

I've teased the boys about how little credit I get, but I know how much I'm loved and respected. In today's world, many mothers want to be the most important parent, but I honestly believe that with boys the father has to have the final say. If women had any sense, they'd realize they had the easy job of being the "good guy."

I haven't always been the most honest person in the world. I don't like to upset people or make them mad. I like everyone to be happy even if I'm not. I don't like confrontation.

With Ron, what you see is what you get. You may not like or agree with what Ron says, but you can take it to the bank because he tells you exactly what he thinks or what he intends to do. The boys don't always like what he says, but they know it's the truth and nothing but the truth. And when they get a compliment they know they've earned it. When Ron was coaching Pop Warner football he didn't make Chance the quarterback (much to my dismay) because someone else was better. When Ron began helping with Little League some of the boys were at our house, and one little guy just assumed that Grant would be the pitcher because "the coach's son is always the pitcher."

It wasn't that way in the Wistrom house. The boys knew if their dad were coach, they'd play because they were the best at that position. And isn't that what we all want? To be rewarded because of what we do, not who we are.

Coaches often make that mistake, especially youth coaches. They aren't totally honest with kids. Kids can take the honesty if you're really being honest. They can handle the brutal truth if you're fair with them. You can go to any varsity football player, and he can tell you who should be playing where and why. Players know who REALLY hustles, even when the coach isn't around. They know whom they can count on and who gets going when the going gets tough.

Kids don't play politics and often coaches do. Coaches will tell parents and kids that if they hustle, work hard, and FOLLOW THE RULES, they'll play. Then some hotshot comes along who breaks all the rules, but he's the secret ingredient to winning the game and, guess what, he starts. If a coach takes a stand then they need to follow through with what they say because the players see through it first.

Of course if it's a program where you win at all costs, then the coach may have a problem, and that's where the parents and system need to support him. Kids need to know that following the rules and respecting authority is more important than winning. And coaches need to be honest about what they expect from their players. Sometimes a player needs another chance, but if he keeps blowing it, then is he learning anything? And what are the other players learning? Coach's rules only apply to the average player; the superstars can do anything they want. Of course this is the same philosophy today's society is debating.

Young people want rules, as long as you're honest about the rules and consequences and make sure the same rules apply to everyone. Set goals, limits, and expectations, but be honest about the rewards and punishments. A coach or a parent can be tough, if you're honest. Don't change the rules halfway through the game, and make sure you follow through on what you say, whether it's a punishment or a reward.

We, as adults, expect children to be honest, and then the adults they respect the most are dishonest with them. Children are the most honest creatures in the world. So where do they learn to be dishonest? I wonder?

I

INDEPENDENCE

It's been very difficult for me to "let go" of my babies. Even today, I want to take charge of their lives, plan their futures, solve their problems. It hasn't been easy for me to let them make mistakes; I want to tell them what to do because I've been through it, and I know what's best for them. Now that they are all gone, the most difficult thing has been letting go. I still want to be the center of their lives as they are ours, but that isn't the case. Makes sense, doesn't it, since I'm the MOM!

They each have a life that involves us, but they have lives beyond us, other priorities. At times, if I allow myself some self-pity, I can become depressed about how independent they've become. Of course that's what parents want for their children, but at times, I am sorry they aren't more dependent on us, like they were as children.

When they were little I did rescue them although Ron didn't like it. He felt that they would never stand on their own if we didn't let them fall down once and a while. I'm not sure who's right or wrong about this issue. I only know that I flew up to the high school when Chance forgot his football helmet, and I've bailed all the boys out when it came to late night school projects. I felt that they were good kids and if their mother didn't help them, then who would?

Oddly enough, the areas where Ron didn't want them to be so independent pertained to their appearances. Ron had a very difficult time dealing with clothing and hair styles, pierced ears and tattoos. While I, on the other hand who has been bleaching my hair since 12, had no problem whatsoever. Finally Ron realized that there were too many important battles to fight to worry about a shaved head or an earring. So the boys were in charge of their clothing decisions at an early age. They had to follow the school dress code, but after that they were pretty much on their own.

When Tracey and his teammates shaved their heads before a big basketball game, some of the parents were horrified. But it didn't take Tracey long to realize he looked so "U-G-L-Y, YOU AIN'T GOT NO ALIBI, YOU UGLY' that we knew he wouldn't do it again for quite some time, if ever.

Kids want to express their independence, and as long as it doesn't bother others, we decided not to make an issue of it. When Chance wanted to get his ear pierced in college, he was worried

about what his dad would say. In order to save face because Ron really didn't want to make anything of it but everyone expected him to, Ron told Chance he'd give him the OK when Chance got his first sack. That way they both won. Sometimes the old boy is pretty sharp! Remember, there are too many issues your children will confront you with. Why not let them win a few small battles, and you worry about the war.

Another way we helped the boys develop independence concerned making them face adults when they had a problem. If they

Dee and the boys

didn't think the coach was being fair then they had to go to him and discuss it. If they had a problem with a teacher then it was their problem. And they did have teachers and coaches who didn't treat them fairly, but we never intervened. I wanted to, plenty of times. But Ron was right. If they were going to make it in this world, we wouldn't always be around to protect them or bail them out of a mess. There would always be problems with others, and they needed to learn to deal with those relationships. Maybe parents are right to step in if things aren't quite fair, but I don't believe it really helps kids in the long run. Our boys learned to talk one-on-one with adults. They learned that right isn't always right, but that's the way life is, and you have to deal with it.

Today all three boys are very independent and they became that way in spite of me. They went away to college and made it on their own. In fact, I think they're too independent. Sometimes I wish they needed the security of Mom and Dad. But I do know parents who have made their children feel that they have to stay close to Mom and Dad because they haven't learned to stand on their own. When we moved from Florida back to Webb City, the boys thought we had moved to the end of the world. You can imagine living in the "magic kingdom" and moving to a little town that didn't even have a movie theater! They all talked about moving back when they were old enough to make there own decisions. Chance knew as soon as he graduated from college, he was returning to Florida to make a lot of money. He'd shake the dust of his shoes and head back to the sunny beaches.

Guess what? Something happened; he grew up. He began to understand the appeal of a small town where everyone knows everyone else and yes, everyone's business. He's chosen to settle in another small town similar to Webb City. He hopes to raise his family there, and while I wish he were still living in the house he built behind ours, I realize the importance of him "being on his own." Grant and Tracey both want to return to the area and coach with their brother. Nothing would make me happier.

But what I'm most proud of is that they've been on their own. They know they can make it without Mom and Dad. They've had a chance to see the other Webb Cities, and they think, right now anyway, that this is where they want to settle.

I can remember watching Chance drive off that first morning he left for college. He wasn't even 18, and his eyes were filled with tears, as were Ron's and mine. I couldn't protect him anymore. I couldn't make all his "ouchies" go away. Then Grant left, then Tracey. Being involved in football, they didn't get to come home much, and Grant and Trace were and are still away at games during

Christmas. They made friends, have summer jobs, and work out during the summers. Sometimes I envy others when their kids come home, but this is just the way it was and is in our family. So I'm thankful that our boys are able to successfully deal with the situations they've had to face. I'm also thankful that they still love to come home, and they still ask for advice even if it's just to make me think they need it!

Oddly enough this has been the most difficult on Ron, who made them so independent. He loves his boys with his heart and soul; they're his best friends. If he could, he'd build a compound and all the boys and their families could live together, with us, just like the Cartrights on the Ponderosa! What's more important is that the boys still think of Ron as their best friend. They still listen, they still ask, and they still respect him. They may not take his advice, but they ask.

So parents, encourage your children to be on their own. Let them try their wings. We may want to keep them close to home where we can protect them, but they need to learn they can survive on their own. You just have to trust that you've given them everything they need to be successful, and then you have to let go. This doesn't mean you can't help them when they ask. It just means you shouldn't make them feel that they can't make it without you, or you can't make it without them. I've found as I grow older that "independence" is something I'm having to learn.

J
JEALOUSY

The question that I am asked the most is, "Are the boys jealous of each other?" I think it would be understandable if they were; however, I honestly believe they all share in each other's success without any envy. Oh, I'm sure Chance would have loved to have played football at Nebraska, but then he wouldn't have met Dee, his wife, at Central Missouri State University. And I'm sure that makes up for any "what ifs" Chance might have had. And, if we're all honest, I know anyone would like Grant's lifestyle, being financially secure at 25.

Grant and his pet snake

As for the money issue, which is what most people wonder about, Grant was and is very generous. As the entire world knows he paid off my credit cards, and he bought his dad a car. I'm sure Grant would do anything for Chance and Tracey, but he and his brothers seem to know there's a fine line there, and they're careful about crossing it. I think Tracey did try to shame Grant into buying a hot tub for him; however, Grant was quick to point out that HE didn't have a hot tub in college, so he was certain that Tracey didn't need one!

But, jealousy has never seemed to be a problem. Actually Grant and Trace seem a little envious of Chance right now. He's married to a beautiful woman who shares his passion for sports and the outdoors, and he's doing exactly what they both want to do some day - coach and live in a small town close to fishing and hunting.

Now, believe me, they still argue, disagree, and wrestle. And they still love to upset me by saying, "He's always been your favorite". To which I always comment, "Yes, he is!!" But they don't argue over "You've got more than I do," unless it's over food!

Ron and I tried to be very careful about handling each boy's success no matter how big or small it may have been. We tried to make each boy feel that his success was the most important at that time, and we never compared what one was doing to what the other two were accomplishing. Whoever was playing at that moment and time got all our attention. It didn't matter whether it was the Super Bowl or Chance's high school football game. One was and is just as important as the other. Now that Grant is playing on Sunday, and Tracey is still on Saturday, we always go to Trace's game, wherever it is. Then if we can, we go to Grant's. We made all three of the boys' college games, so that's the way we intend to finish Tracey's career.

When Chance played college football, Grant was five years younger, and we had no idea if he would achieve the same success.

The Family with Meathead, the dog who bit Bill Walsh

So we never really discussed where Grant might play. By his senior year in high school, Grant was being recruited by several major colleges, and we didn't make a big deal of it because what really mattered was that Chance got a college degree, whether he played football at a Division I or Division II college. When Grant signed with Nebraska, he always credited Chance for helping him become the player he was and is. Both Tracey and Grant say that between listening to Ron and watching Chance, they had the best mentors a boy could have. Even today, although Grant is at the professional level, he still discusses his "job" with Chance.

Tracey has been able to pick the brains of both his older brothers and learn from their mistakes. The boys call each other several times a week, and they usually know more about what's going on with each other than Ron and I do. This is probably one of the things I'm most proud of, the love they feel for each other. Chance had Ron as his best man at his wedding, and Grant and Trace were groomsmen, and I think that says it all!

K
KEYS - as in Florida

V-A-C-A-T-I-O-N in the Summer Time or so the song goes. We were never able to take vacations when normal people did because the boys had baseball or football camps, so we usually took our trips during spring break. In fact, until we moved to Florida we never really took vacations, how-ever, in Florida, we discovered the Keys. I probably should have written this chapter under Magic Moments as those days were truly magical.

The first year we went there we discovered some small cot-tages right on the Gulf that were very reasonable. The following year we bought a small dinghy and loaded it on top of our regular ski boat and headed for the Keys.

At first I started doing my thing by finding all kinds of places we could take the boys.

Tracey in the Keys

Once again Ron reminded me that I should let the boys decide what they wanted to do. And what was that? They were perfectly happy fishing, swimming, and just being little Tom Sawyers! They would don their life jackets, pack snacks, grab their fishing poles, load up the dinghy, and head out to "sea."

We had painted the dinghy a bright yellow, so we could see them wherever they were. We also had walkie-talkie so we were always in contact with them. Of course, the Gulf is very shallow so you can almost walk across it. Needless to say, the boys felt like they were on an adventure to end all adventures. Chance was in

Ron and Tracey in the Keys

charge of the crew, and while there may have been some fights, we never heard about them. That was the great thing about the system. The boys knew that as long as we didn't find out about the fights, they could keep doing their own thing. So no one ever told about any problems. They were just like "Three Men in a Tub!"

When they got tired or the water was a little rough, they would come in and fish from the pier. As young as Tracey was, he would fight the pelicans for every little fish he reeled to shore. We promised the boys that whatever they caught, we'd cook. And they caught everything from stingray to octopus to shark and we ate it!!! The boys loved it.

On several occasions Gammy and Grandpa went with us, and those memories are probably some of the best times we ever had. And we didn't even see a football game!

The point of all this is that kids don't really need to go to Disney World every other year or see every tourist attraction on the map. I don't think our boys are the exception to the rule. Kids want to spend time with the people they love. They want to do what they enjoy doing. I personally don't think most kids enjoy waiting in long lines for a four-minute ride. I don't think they care about eating out, especially if they have to wait and the meal takes a long time.

The times our boys remember are those times Ron threw them in the pool or went fishing with them. In Florida, the times they talk aren't about Disney World or Sea World. They remember the days we spent catching crabs with our fishing poles and chicken wings. The laugh about the fights they had in the dinghy, and how they were always smiling by the time they returned to shore.

What about us? What did we do? Did Ron and I have a good time? What do you think? Imagine, lying on a quiet, private sandy beach listening to Ragae bands, sipping a tropical drink, watching your little darlings having a great time - close enough we could see them, but far enough away that we couldn't hear them! They even furnished dinner! And it all cost MUCH less that taking a family of five to Disney World for two days! Can you imagine that paradise could be any better?

So parents, ask your kids what they want to do. Sure you may have to plan things better because it won't be planned for you. Yes, you'll probably spend more time with your children, and it will be quality time because you'll be doing more than just standing in line with them. It really doesn't cost a lot of money to give your children memories that they will never forget.

My advice would be to wait and make those visits to places like Disney World when they're old enough to be dropped off at the gate and picked up later. Besides, they'll probably have a much better time, and so will you!

L
LOVE

Parents, if you can't help your kids in sports, or you can't afford to send them to every camp that comes along, then love them. Love them unconditionally. Love them enough to make rules, and stay home to see that they're obeyed. Love them enough to get them to practice on time if that's what they want. Love them when you don't think they deserve your love. Don't be afraid to hug them and kiss them, even if they act like they don't like it. Who cares? You're the boss.

Enjoy your children. Don't be in a hurry for them to grow up. Enjoy their friends. Let them know they're welcome at your house, but set rules and expect everyone to follow them. We never had problems with kids tearing up the house or causing trouble because they knew Ron would make their lives miserable. And they respected him because he was the same guy who took time to shoot baskets with them in the driveway or throw the football to them in the pool. Ron treated all the kids the way he treated our kids, and they loved it.

My life was never happier than when we had a house full of boys, all ages, laughing and goofing off. So what if the house gets messy, or soda pop gets spilled on the floor. It all cleans up, and when the kids are gone, you can clean the house. I won't say that it will stay that way, even when the kids leave, because my house certainly doesn't. Just think, at least if you have kids around all of the time, you have an excuse for a messy house.

Laugh with your kids, not at them. Although I must admit we've laughed a lot about what the kids have done. At times we laughed at them, but they've certainly laughed at me enough. So it worked. Even today, everyone teases each other. There is no mercy. If Chance does something stupid, Grant and Trace will never let him forget it. And the same holds true for the other two. Unless there's blood, anything goes. Once Chance was in a fight on his way home from a football game, and once we found out he was OK, I'm ashamed to admit it, but we had a good laugh about it!

I was on my way to cook Grant's favorite taco recipe on TV this year when I had a terrible wreck. As soon as Chance saw I wasn't on TV, he knew something was terribly wrong. He knew I'd never miss a chance to be on TV. Ron assured him I was OK, but he wanted to see for himself.

I looked like the Elephant Man, and yet I only had a few cracked ribs. Even the doctor was amazed. I had to have a CAT scan and an MRI. When the doctor showed the boys the x-ray of my head, he commented that "As you can see, there's nothing up there." Well, that brought the house down. Ron and Chance had several comments to make. The doctor responded by saying that I really was "one tough lady."

We're a sick bunch, aren't we?

Having children has been the most exciting and rewarding experience Ron and I have ever shared. I can't imagine what our lives would have been like without them. You should feel the same way about your babies. If you don't, it's probably your fault. You're the adult. You should know what to do. If all else fails, then love them. Love can open a lot of doors.

M
MEDIA

If your child is considering playing college ball, then be prepared for the MEDIA. I always thought that if you read it or saw it on television, it must be true. I've found that isn't always the case.

The media have been very good to our boys. I've often thought that perhaps the boys received too much publicity as I know that parents, especially mothers, get sick of seeing the same kids mentioned over and over in the paper. But, I also know that there may not be a lot of news happening in a small town, so when they have someone who is drawing national attention, it becomes newsworthy. I know that offensive and defensive linemen are often ignored, and if it weren't for them there either would or wouldn't be any points scored. So every now and then it would be nice just to feature them in the headlines. (Chance played offense in Florida, and it used to really tick me off that his name was seldom mentioned!)

It's great to have a local paper that covers everything from kindergarten to high school in the sports section because every child should see his name and picture in the paper.

But once a young man moves to a higher level, then anything goes. I know if Grant or Trace had done some of the same things that other boys their age might do, their names would be on the air coast-to-coast. Yes, I do think they should behave better because of their positions; however, they are still just young men, and they will make mistakes, like anyone else their age.

Once when Grant was at Nebraska, someone told me that they had heard on national television that he had been picked up for stealing. I was devastated. Ron didn't believe it, and Chance was outraged. He said if Grant had taken anything it was probably something like an old couch off another player's porch. If he had been any other kid, the media would have ignored him, but since Grant was a high profile player, the event was blown out of proportion. The truth is it never happened. I don't know what was on television, or if it really was Grant's name. It just shows you that there will always be people who want to believe the worst. People who are just waiting for someone to fail, so that they can say, "See I knew he wasn't that good of a kid."

I am constantly telling the boys that people are always watching them and judging them. The media only give the public what they want to see or read. The best way to be happy with what the media write about you is to only give them good things to say.

Grant's banner on Senior Day at Nebraska

Don't do anything wrong that would be newsworthy. Be boring or just do nice things.

When Grant was going through the NFL draft, it made me furious to hear the hosts on sports' radio discuss how Grant was a bust. They seem to forget that he was a young man, not even 21, who had a family listening. I know it's all part of the entire sports' scene, but it still upsets me. I would like to tell parents of future NFL players not to listen to what is said, because no one really knows what a player is going to do. As the number six pick in the first round, there were many who complained that the Rams should have picked another player. Those same people should go back and see who was drafted ahead of Grant and where they are today. Personally, I think the Rams got their money's worth!

Coming from Webb City, a small town outside of Joplin, the local media do a great job of covering all of the boys from this area. They've followed Tracey to Nebraska, Grant to St. Louis, and Chance to Seneca. At one of the Nebraska games, they put a microphone on Ron to catch his comments. What they didn't know is that

Ron is very quiet during the game. You can't tell from his expression whether we're winning or losing.

On the other hand, I am VERY vocal. The problem is I don't always know what I'm talking about. One of our local cameramen, who knows us pretty well, said he knew the minute he saw the tape that they had wired the wrong Wistrom! The television and print media have followed us on road trips, and they've always been very generous with their comments. They've honored our privacy, and when we've told them things off the record, they've kept them OFF THE RECORD.

In chapter "N" I talk about what happened to Grant at the pizza place. Many people didn't even hear about it because the local media did not make a big thing about it. One news director even called us and told us that he had told his people that he didn't want it mentioned because he knew Grant, and he knew there must be more to the story. Ron and I are still very appreciative of the concern they showed to Grant and our family. In return, we try to be very gracious to that station. It's times like that I'm glad I live in small, midwest community.

The media are like a double-edged sword. I love it when they say good things about the boys, and I'm like a stuck pig when they say something with which I don't agree, even if it's somewhat true! I guess mothers are just that way.

The main thing I wish the media would remember is that everyone should be treated the same. Of course, no one cares what I wore to the Super Bowl game, but there were a lot of cameras on Kurt Warner's wife. People, including me, like to know what the rich and famous are doing. I'm ashamed to admit it, but I buy the Enquirer because I'm interested in who does what. I guess I'm a hypocrite, but I have learned not to believe everything I read. I hope people remember that rule.

I also hope if my children ever do anything to make national news that people will remember there are always two sides to each story, and if what's written or said isn't true, I hope the media report that as well.

One more thing for the record: Ron doesn't really enjoy being interviewed. I, on the other hand, welcome phone calls, interviews, news stories, everything. (Sorry, but the boys take after their dad on that issue.)

N

NEVER SAY NEVER

If you're a parent, "never say never" when referring to your children. I always thought that I followed that strategy; however, Ron and I were returning from the Big 12 game during Grant's senior year when I ignored my own advice. We were right around Dallas, and I reached over and took Ron's hand. I was feeling pretty smug about myself and my life.

"Yes, sirree," I thought, "we've done pretty well for ourselves. Who would have ever thought that all the boys would go to college on scholarships. One would be going to the NFL. They were good boys, never gave us any trouble. Ron and I have certainly done a darn good job as parents!" Then I was dumb enough to say it aloud.

Honestly, I never think, and I certainly don't say those things. I know you can go from the penthouse to the outhouse in the snap of the fingers! And that's exactly what happened.

Ron and I got home about 12:30 am, and we were sitting there patting ourselves on the back when the phone rang. You know the sound! The one that tells you something BIG is wrong because no one ever calls that late unless something BIG is wrong. We heard Grant's voice on the other end.

"Mom, I've got something to tell you."

My heart dropped to my feet.

It seems that Grant returned from the Big 12 game and went to a pizza place. Some guy was giving his girlfriend a bad time, and Grant told him to quit. One thing led to another, and the guy punched Grant. Grant fell into a chair, and he just sat there.

Later when all the boys were discussing this, Chance laughed about why Grant let the guy hit him twice. Once, Chance could understand, but twice? (In our house you never get any sympathy!) Grant said he was smart enough to know that if he hit the guy, his name would be all over the news. Even though he was defending a girl, he knew that a lot of people would believe the worst. I'm very proud of Grant that he was able to think about that so quickly, especially after being punched.

Back to the story. Someone called the police, and they said that even though there were witnesses who collaborated Grant's story that he didn't do a thing, the police would still have to write-up everyone who was involved. Now, I know if Grant had not been a Husker, everyone would have probably just been warned. Personally I think the other guy should have been charged, but everyone is always saying that football players get off the hook, so Grant paid the price.

When all the facts were given, the charges were dropped. Coach Osborne even called to tell us that he believed Grant, and from what he had found out Grant was completely innocent. To Ron, the damage was done. Soon we learned that while the charges were dropped, this incident is probably still on file at the Lincoln Police Department. Although Grant was completely innocent, hav-

Tracey and Grant ready to square off

ing the charges dropped did not prove his innocence; therefore, it's public knowledge that charges were filed against Grant.

When Grant went to the Super Bowl, his name was listed in an article as one of the Super Bowl players who had had a problem with the law! Now, does that seem fair? Someone will see or hear that and assume that Grant is just another bad apple in the NFL. I would love to do something about it, But Grant says we know the truth. Those who want to believe it, will elieve it. Nothing can change that.

Wait, this story isn't finished. If the phone call from Grant wasn't bad enough, the phone rang about an hour later. This time it was Tracey. I proceeded to tell him that we knew what had happened to Grant.

And he said, "Grant, what happened to Grant?"

Then I knew we were in big trouble because obviously Trace had a pretty important reason to call us that late.

He proceeded to tell us how he and his friend had been to a party, and basically they had been chased and roughed up a little. No, he hadn't been picked up by the police because he wasn't anybody, just a red-shirt freshman. The main reason he was calling was that he had broken his glasses, and he needed to get them fixed as soon as possible. He assured me that he was in much better shape then his friend. At least no one had taken Tracey's shoes or clothes! I'm convinced if someone had found out that he was Grant Wistrom's little brother, it might have made the news. Just imagine, two Wistroms in jail at the same time! What a story!

Ron must have aged at least ten years that night!

If there's a chance that your child will be in the spotlight, remind him that at any point in time, he can lose it all. What might seem perfectly innocent at the time can come back to haunt him years later. Life can change in an instant, and just when you think you've got the world on a string, the string can break, and everything can fall down around you.

So parents, NEVER SAY NEVER!!!

O

OSBORNE

When I came to O, I thought of Oprah because I'm hoping she will read this. While I may not make the Oprah Book Club, maybe she will invite me to discuss the boys on one of her Raising Good Kids segments!

As I sat pondering what I might wear on TV that would make me look thin, I glanced over at the bookcase and saw one of Tom Osborne's books, *On Solid Ground*. What could be better in a book about raising football players than a chapter on Tom Osborne?

Coach Osborne, Ron, Coach Thompson

Tom Osborne was everything a parent and player would want in a coach. As I mentioned before, when Grant was being recruited, I had no idea who T.O. was. Nebraska didn't have the razzle, dazzle of a Notre Dame and Lou Holtz. I had been raised on Barry Switzer and Oklahoma. Having lived in Florida, I was a big Bobby Bowden fan, and because of Joe Montana I knew about Bill Walsh.

But when Tom Osborne called I actually didn't know who he was or where he coached.

On the other hand Ron thought he was the King of College Football. Even today, when Ron talks about T.O. there is a reference in his voice. Coach Osborne is a man of integrity, and he exemplified that to his players.

I have to admit after meeting Coach Osborne that I, too, was impressed with his presence. He has a sincere warmth about him that makes you feel as if you are the most important person at that moment in time. And frankly, I think that at that moment YOU are Coach Osborne's main concern.

When your son is being recruited, remember the head coach will be the closest thing to a parent your child will have for four or five years. You want to make sure it's someone you feel really cares about your child. We were very fortunate that Chance went to Central Missouri State Universtiy in Warrensburg, Missouri, where he, too, had coaches like Terry Noland and Jeff Floyd who really cared about their players.

When Ron and I took Grant back to Nebraska for his second visit, a young man drove me to the mall while Ron visited Nebraska's weight room. I asked my young driver all about Nebraska and Coach Osborne. You could hear the admiration and love in his voice as he talked about his head coach. He was a walk-on, no scholarship or money, just a young man who wanted to be a part of the Nebraska program. He continued to tell me how proud he was to be on Tom Osborne's team. He talked about how T.O. knew all the players, whether they were All-Americans or a walk-on, as he was. Osborne knew their names and tried to talk to each one before the game, even if it was just to say "Good luck." Now I don't know if all young men felt this way, but the one I visited with certainly did.

That's one of the amazing things about Nebraska football. They have so many walk-ons! Kids who were high school All-Americans and could probably start at most colleges with full scholarships are willing to "walk-on" at Nebraska without any compensation. These young men just want to be a part of the Big Red Machine.

That night, Ron and I went to a small get-together at Osborne's house. I was surprised to see that the king of Nebraska football lived in a modest home, nothing overwhelming, just comfortable. His wife, Nancy, was just as charming and kind as everyone had said. We left feeling that our baby boy would be well taken care of at Nebraska!

During our visit, one of the interesting things we noticed about Coach Osborne and the other Nebraska coaches was that they made no promises about either Grant or Tracey and their time at NU. They were offered a scholarship and a chance to play football, but there were no guarantees. Other coaches and recruiters had promised far more than that! One coach told Grant that he would change his entire defense to suit Grant's style. Another recruiter promised Grant that he would have a NFL career if he went to "his" school.

Coach Osborne and his staff were completely honest with us. He told us that Grant would have every opportunity to play, but he couldn't make any promises. He did promise if Grant got hurt and couldn't play football that Nebraska would still honor his scholarship. No, he couldn't promise him an NFL career, and parents, no one else can guarantee that for your child; however, he introduced us to Grant's position coach, Tony Samuels, who had produced several NFL players.

And guess what? Tom Osborne and his staff were true to their word. Grant and Tracey have had every opportunity to prove what they can do both on and off of the field. In my opinion they've had the best coaches in college football, the best facilities, the best education, the best fans, and more. As you can tell Ron and I are sold on Nebraska.

The only time Coach Osborne really discussed the NFL with Grant was at the end of Grant's junior year when everyone was telling Grant that he should leave and prepare for the draft. Several

Nebraska Fans in San Diego

of the NFL draft watchers listed Grant as an early draft pick. When that starts happening, it does become difficult for a young man to see past the money issue. There's always that chance that he can get hurt during his senior year and there goes his shot at a pro career.

As parents, we weren't prepared to see our son thrown into the NFL lifestyle. Of course the coaches didn't want him to leave either. Yet, Tom Osborne never tried to influence Grant one way or the other. When Ron and Grant met with T.O., the only thing Osborne offered to do was give Grant some names of people whom he felt would be able to give Grant enough information for him to make an intelligent decision. Coach Osborne just gave Grant access to people who could discuss his options; not once did he advise him. That meeting probably sealed Ron's opinion of Tom Osborne as an honest coach who truly cares about his players and their futures. Grant decided to stay and he has never regretted his decision. The rest is Big Red history.

When Tracey was being recruited, several coaches came to Webb City including Gary Barnett from Northwestern. Trace had visited Northwestern, and he really liked the players and the program. Grant told Coach Osborne that he shouldn't assume that Trace would go to Nebraska just because Grant had. In fact, the opposite was probably true. I'm sure that Coach Osborne was hoping he could scratch one visit since it was obvious that Trace knew all about the program. However, he also realized that it was important to let Tracey know that NU wanted him as much as they had wanted Grant. So, he made another trip to southwestern Missouri to visit Trace. I think Tracey appreciated it, and I know Ron and I did. I don't know how we would have made the journey to both Nebraska AND Northwestern!

Besides being a coach, Tom Osborne was a father figure to a lot

Grant, Kathy, Ron, Tracey at the boysfirst practice together at Nebraska

of his players. Our boys didn't really need one as I'm sure they felt they had way more father than they needed, and they would have gladly shared some of Ron's fatherly advice with their friends. But, there are many young athletes who do need someone to set the rules and draw the lines. Coach Osborne and his staff did that. Personally, Ron and I don't care what anyone says, Coach Osborne held his players accountable for their behavior. TV stations, talk show hosts, whoever can say whatever they want, in my opinion, T.O. always put the player and what was best for him above the win.

People still argue about Lawrence Phillips, but I believe in my heart that Tom Osborne wanted to help Lawrence reach his full potential. I'm sure that certain radio sports' figures will rip that one a part. Yes, Lawrence blew it. He threw it all away. But it seems to me that the only stability he had in his adult life was Tom Osborne. I'll agree that Lawrence was a great football player, and of course T.O. wanted him to do well for the good of the team. Beyond that, no one will ever convince me that it was all for football. Maybe it has to do with ego. Coaches don't want to admit they've made a mistake. Whatever it was, Coach Osborne cares about Lawrence Phillips as he cares about all his players. Notice I used present tense because even today I believe that Tom Osborne would try to help his former players if he could. Call me the eternal goody-two-shoes, but I feel that strongly about Coach Osborne. I've listened to my boys and other players discuss him, and I've never heard a derogatory statement made about the man. As I heard Grant once say, "I don't know what it is about the man, but you don't want him mad at you. You don't want to disappoint him."

Ron and I were very disappointed when Osborne left football. He still had so much to offer, and yet that last year may have been the straw that broke the camel's back.

One must admit, however, that the political arena isn't much different than the football field. T.O. is still dealing with egos, peoplel of varying backgrounds, etc. He's still working to make everyone come together for a common goal. Perhaps the big difference is that when grown men, as compared to young football players, make mistakes, the public is more willing to forgive and forget.

T.O. you've got your work cut out for you, dag gum it!

P

PRIDE

"Pride goeth before the fall." There's a very fine line between making your children feel self-confident and turning them into arrogant little show-offs! That's where parents need to take over. Children need to be taught that it's a lot easier to fall from a pedestal than to ever reach the top of one. They need to be aware of those who are less fortunate, and kids need to learn to downplay their successes.

Of course, if we parents sit in the stands and yell about the other players or boast about our children, than it's very difficult to expect our children to do otherwise. However, if we are quick to acknowledge others' abilities and triumphs, than our children will follow. If someone is really good at what he does than he doesn't have to brag about himself because everyone knows it. If a young man is a great football player then his dad doesn't have to tell the coach because everyone else will. Truly great players are often great in spite of their parents!

Young football players need to be taught to be gracious about their talents. They need to be polite and say, "thank you" when someone acknowledges their performances. Don't ignore the little guy waiting for your autograph, and don't make fun of those players who aren't as good as you. Next year they may pass you by!

When a child starts to believe everything he sees or reads about himself, then he may stop trying to get better and become satisfied with past performances. Eventually, someone comes along who is bigger, better, faster, and stronger! As difficult as it is, it is up to the parents to keep a child from thinking he's better than anyone else. It's easy, as parents, to get caught up in all the excitement of state championships, and other successes. As a mother, I loved reading all the wonderful things people would say about the boys. I actually started believing it. But I soon found that the media can be very fickle, so, if I chose to ignore the negative things written or said about the boys, than I had to ignore the glowing remarks that were made.

Ron and the boys were far better about not getting excited about either positive or negative comments. They seemed to better understand the nature of the beast. I, on the other hand, often wanted to send thank you notes to reporters or VOICE MY OPINIONS to late night sports radio hosts who referred to Grant as a "bust!" Perhaps it's easy in high school to believe all the things that small towns feel about high school heroes, but a player is much better off if he understands that it's all part of the game. Enjoy what you hear or read, but don't believe it!

And if all else fails, then getting together with your brothers will usually put things into perspective. When the boys are at home, they're just C-Dub, Boog, and Baby Trace. Having brothers who know all your shortcomings and will be glad to take advantage of them can usually control getting a "big" head!

Chance, Tracey, Grant in the Virgin Islands

Q
QUESTIONS

There are several questions that I have been asked over and over. Here are some of the more frequent ones.

Q. What's it like to have a son who is a professional football player?

A. I don't think I appreciate it as much as Ron does since he understands the game more than I do. To me, Grant has a job that he loves, and he gets well paid for his work. Don't get me wrong, I've enjoyed the perks as much as Grant. I love going to the games and seeing his name on the big screen, but I don't feel that I've ever really absorbed everything. At times I'm still overwhelmed by the idea that Grant is "one of those guys" the boys used to idolize on Monday Night Football. There are even times when I wish Grant had a "normal" job, which allowed him to live a "normal" life. When you get right down to it, Grant isn't much different than most 26-year olds, he's just able to buy more toys.

Q. Why don't you and Grant make Chunky Soup commercials?

A. I'm so glad you asked! I would love to make Chunky Soup commercials with Grant. If anyone is listening, I am available for all promotional events. The problem is that Grant is pretty busy. However, I would certainly work around my schedule. I'm available for speaking engagements, I can tell humorous stories, and I would be more than happy to fall from the baggage compartment of an airplane.

At one point Grant and I were the spokespersons for Ott's Foods which is a great little company in Carthage, Missouri, that makes barbecue sauce and salad dressings. I loved making personal appearances, but Grant really didn't have the time to make so many weekend stops, so my career came to a halt. It was actually at one of the Ott's promotional signings that several women asked why I didn't write a book about raising three boys around football. And here we are today. (I also have a GREAT idea for a Harley commercial!!)

Q. Are the boys jealous of each other?
A. NO, NO, NO. See the chapter on jealousy

Q. You and Ron don't have to worry about anything, now that Grant's a professional football player, do you?
A. Despite what everyone thinks, Grant is not supporting anyone in the Wistrom household. Yes, he bought Ron a car and paid off my credit cards. I'm sure if we really needed anything, he would help us, but so would Chance and Tracey. Grant has his life, and we all have ours. I'm still teaching and will probably die at my desk because of the retirement rules, and Ron works tirelessly in our development. It bothers Ron that people believe Grant is supporting us, but I don't really care because people believe what they want to believe.

Q. Just how high were your credit cards?
A. Only Grant and I know for sure, and I've threatened him with a tell-all book if he ever divulges the information! They were the accumulation of many years of football trips from California to New York! Grant continues to tell me that he doesn't intend to bail me out again!

Q. Why didn't Grant go to the Kansas City Chiefs?
A. Those of you who "know" football know the answer. But, for those of you, like me, who don't understand how the draft works, Grant didn't really have a choice about where he went. He had to go where he was drafted. He couldn't negotiate the place where he played. Fortunately, St. Louis has been good to Grant, and he's very happy playing for the Rams. It was truly a good

match!

Q. Would Tracey like to play professional ball?

A. Tracey doesn't say much because he doesn't like people to compare him to Grant. However, I believe that any one who loves football would like to play in the NFL!

Grant on Draft Day

Q. What do Tracey and Grant want to do when they're done with football?

A. They both say that they would like to teach and coach with Chance. They've got it all worked out that Chance would be the head coach, Grant would coach a defensive position, and Tracey would coach an offensive position. (And Mom would like for them to be close to Webb City! What a dream come true for me!)

Q. Just how much did you have to cook when they were all at home?

A. Anyone who has boys knows that food is very important. It didn't seem like a big thing when all the boys were at home. But, now that the boys have left, I've almost forgotten what it was like. Thinking back, I can remember cooking 2-3 pounds of hamburger plus 6-8 pork chops for the meat dish. I fixed a lot of potatoes and pasta!

Q. Was Grant always a good football player?

A. Grant had to work and practice to get where he is today. The coaches always pushed Grant to work harder. Once, when he was in tenth grade, the coaches didn't think that he was hustling, so they made him stand under the goal post through the entire practice. Grant said that balls were bouncing off of him, and kids would run into him. He said it was one of the worst days of his life, and he wanted to quit. But, he knew he'd better not complain or tell Dad because he'd get in more trouble for not hustling. Now, his coaches have told us that they knew if they could get Grant mad he'd work harder. They also knew that Ron wouldn't get mad at them like some parents would. During one season, they didn't start Grant although they've told us they knew they should have. It made him work harder and longer to get a starting position. I didn't think that was the right thing to do, but maybe Grant wouldn't have been as good as he is now if those coaches hadn't kept on his case.

Q. Did the boys fight when they were little?

A. Does the sun rise in the east? They fought like cats and dogs. It was the usual "he's looking at me, he touched me, he's thinking about me." But they wouldn't let anyone else pick on each other. They're still very proctective of each other.

Q. Will Grant stay in St. Louis?

A. Grant loves St. Louis. I'm sure he would like to finish his career there. However, the NFL doesn't work that way. We'll have to wait and see what happens.

Q. What kind of students were the boys?

A. All of the boys were good students. They were smart, but they worked to make good grades because it was expected of them. Grant and Trace were both Academic All Americans, and Chance won the Mackey Award at CMSU for scholarship and leadership.

Q. Your boys were lucky to be so talented, weren't they?

A. I used to comment that our boys had been lucky, but the more I think about it luck had very little to do with it. The boys worked long hours to get where they are today. Our entire family sacrificed a great deal to allow them to be involved in sports. Ron once told me that we make our own luck. I'm beginning to think that he's right. Meeting Ron on a blind date may have been luck, but staying married for 33 years required a lot of hard work! Having a good marriage, raising good kids, it all takes WORK AND COMMITMENT.

Q. Isn't it difficult to sit in the stands and watch the boys? Aren't you worried about them getting hurt?

A. This will sound stupid, but I've never thought about the boys getting hurt. Maybe I'm too dumb to realize how brutal football can be, but I've just always trusted God to take care of them. I'm one of those people who always looks at the bright side. At least I try to do that. My mother always told me that when life gives you lemons, make lemonade. I hope I never have to test that theory when it comes to the boys.

Also, Ron always assured me that the boys could get hurt more in baseball or basketball because they weren't wearing as much padding!

Q. Did the boys play in other sports?

A. All the boys played everything from soccer to wrestling. If kids are involved in sports, they don't have a great deal of time to get in trouble. Ron always felt that being a part of a team is the best thing to prepare kids for the working world. We also found out that college coaches like to recruit kids who are involved in several sports because all sports develop skills and work ethics.

Q. Did the boys have a lot of girlfriends?

A. I could really get into trouble with this one. Personally, I never wanted the boys to go steady because I wanted them to concentrate on school and athletics. In fact, I tell all boys and girls that there are plenty of fish in the sea, and while they're young they shouldn't be tied down to any certain person. Too many things can happen. I never wanted them to go on vacations with girls, and I never really wanted to take anyone with us. It was a personal thing.

Q. Do you think athletes are over paid?

A. No one is worth millions of dollars, but if someone is going to be paid that much, then I'm glad Grant can be one of them. I personally think that they should pay everyone the same, and the players could earn extra money for points scored, tackles, sacks, etc. I also think it's outrageous that they put up with some of these cocky attitudes. I don't care how good they are. It's giving the wrong message to young athletes.

Q. Do you think athletes should be role models?

A. Kids will always admire athletes, whether they deserve it or not. Athletes complain that they didn't ask to be role models. It doesn't matter whether they asked for the job, they have it. They should try to set good examples

R
RELIGION

Probably the area that Ron and I ignored the most was religion, and it is the area with which children might need the most guidance.

Like many young married couples we were often too busy in our lives to make time for God. Oh sure, you're probably saying, "You had time for football, baseball, and other activities. But you didn't have time for the most important coach in the world." And that's right. We believed in God; we knew he died for us; we wanted our family to go to heaven. We felt that being "good" parents was enough.

It isn't.

As a young mother I thought it was my duty to take the boys to church. Ron worked long hours, and he did so many other things that I never pressed the issue. I never wanted the boys to think their dad had any "big" faults, although I knew he did, so I would rationalize that Ron was such a great father that I would handle the Jesus factor. IT SHOULDN'T BE THAT WAY, ESPECIALLY WITH BOYS! They need to see their dad in church. They need to know everyone needs God, even Dad.

I am so grateful to Christ's Church of Oronogo youth ministers (Wade Landers and Greg Corona) who got the boys involved in activities. Then the boys brought me and eventually Ron followed. Forgetting all about football scholarships, championship games, and All-Americans, the most

Family celebrates after state basketball championship

important event in our family concerned all of us being baptized and going to church as a family. It came late in our married life. I sincerely regret that Ron and I didn't realize what going to church as a family would do for us and for the boys.

For the boys to see their father, who they usually saw as someone who was in complete control of his life, acknowledge that yes, he needed God was probably the most important observation they ever made about Ron. For them to know that Ron had faith in God was a turning point in our lives. It really is true that God is in his control, and he knows wha's best for us if we let him take control.

As I said before, I had taken the boys to Sunday school when they were little. But, as they grew older they questioned why they had to go when Dad didn't. Luckily a young man named Wade came along and got Tracey involved at church, and Grant and his friends became active in Fellowship of Christian Athletes. Tracey began to take such an interest in church that I began to worry that maybe it was some kind of cult group. Our neighbors went to church there, and they invited me to their Bible studies. Eventually I went to Sunday services. By this time, I didn't really bug Ron anymore about going, but, as I studied the Bible more I realized that as Christians you really are responsible to lead others to Christ. So I began nagging him again.

At this point in our lives, Ron was working more and more hours at his job. The boys were involved in their own lives, and I began to feel neglected like many women do at this time in their lives. Other major events happened like Ron losing his job, and eventually I turned more and more to prayer to help with our problems. NEVER underestimate the power of prayer. I truly believe that it was prayer that eventually led Ron to church. Losing his job was a devastating blow to Ron as he had given so much of himself to his work. He really thought that he could do it all on his own, and it was difficult for him to admit that he needed anyone, even God.

One Saturday night I had been on Ron's case about going to

church with me. I even went so far as to comment that since he wasn't working, there wasn't any excuse he could use about being tired, so he could certainly get up and go to church with me. Again, he refused. At this point I said to myself, "God, I can't do it anymore. You have to take over." I had made that deal with God before, but this time I felt as if I really couldn't do it any longer. I felt drained from working, adjusting to Ron's not working, and what really bothered me was that I now knew how vital it was for all of us to be in church.

So, finally God had me where He wanted me, on my knees willing to let His will be done. As I've said before, giving up control is very difficult for me. As soon as I turned it over to God, and really meant it, Ron said, "OK, I'll go to church with you tomorrow." And we've been going ever since. I'm sorry to say, but we slack off during football season.

The Wistrom Family

I won't say things have been perfect since then, but things are different. I can't explain it, but there's a peace and contentment that I never knew. Ron is different and the boys see it. They may not be able to describe it, but they can see that our lives have changed. The boys saw their dad lose a job that he didn't deserve to lose, and they saw him turn to God for help. And guess what? Our life just continues to get better and better. Although it appeared that we, as a family, had everything, a piece was missing. We just didn't know what that piece was until we found it.

The missing piece was peace with God. I truly believe that the boys also feel that life is not complete without God's presence in their lives. And I know they use prayer for guidance. Now I'm not foolish enough to think that they don't do things they shouldn't because I do things I shouldn't do. However, I also truly believe that they know what God can do in their lives.

We are responsible for bringing our children to Christ. And I believe it's a sin if we don't, and we will be held accountable if we, as parents, ignore this. When Ron and I stand before God I don't believe He'll judge us on how well the boys played football. I believe we'll be judged on whether or not we made Him the center of our family. I hope we pass!

Again, I feel a knot in my stomach when I think about those years we weren't in church. I had no idea of the impact God could and would make in their lives. I used to always tell the boys that whatever happened, we needed to thank God, because He was in charge! One day, I was alone with the boys, ages one to eight. It was about 100 degrees in downtown Joplin. Ron was in Florida, and the car broke down. Chance looked at me and said, "OK, Mom, let me hear you thank God for this one."

The point is that I did try to bring God into the boys' lives. We prayed together, and I talked to them about being good Christians. I think Ron and I did a great job of teaching the boys to be kind and considerate, to do the right thing. But it wasn't until I began to listen to God's word that I realized how much God wanted to do and would do for us. I didn't really understand the power of prayer until I began to pray with sincerity and passion. I just had no idea how much we had handicapped the boys by ignoring God.

If you really want to know how to help your children become responsible adults, you need to be in church as a family. You need to trust in God's plan. You need to teach your children to pray for God's guidance. When I see a young family sitting together in church, I could almost cry because I have to face the one big mistake we made as a family. The sight also makes me cry because I know how much easier it will be for them to face their problems with God in their corner.

I know the boys will still have problems, although I'd try to solve them if I could. But I also know that they know they can call on God for help. Yes, I would like them to be more involved with a church home. I would like Grant to be one of the players who looks at the camera and points to the heavens. I've talked to him about it, but he knows me pretty well! He said, "Mom, you'd like me to do that because it would look good to the folks in Webb City" And he's right. As I said before we all want our children to look perfect because it reflects on us.

Then he explained to me that I would probably never witness that because it wouldn't be him, and God didn't need anymore hypocrites. As he's told me before, many athletes are very sincere about their testimonies on TV, but he's not comfortable with that image. Yes, God is important to him, and yes, he prays to God for guidance. He's happy to talk to kids about his faith and beliefs, but he's not perfect, and he doesn't want to present himself as someone who has all the answers.

All the boys seem to feel the same way. I suppose they get that from their father, who is one of the most sincerely good and honest men I've ever known. What you see is what you get. There's nothing phony about Ron, and if you don't want the answer, don't ask. That's the way the boys were raised, and, as I said before, sometimes I didn't agree with his brutal honesty. I do realize that just being in church doesn't automatically make you a good Christian.

Ron is probably more of a man of integrity than many men I know who have always attended church. I tend to get caught up in what looks good to others. Ron doesn't, and the boys are more like him in that respect. If you follow the Golden Rule and have your own convictions about right and wrong, then God knows what's in your heart.

Perhaps if we all worried more about impressing God, instead of mankind, we'd be better off. I know I would be. I still believe it's necessary to be aware of the impression you are making, especially if you are in a position to influence others. The boys seemed to have learned if you can't be honest about what you're going say, then keep your mouth shut because the good Lord knows the truth anyway.

I do want the boys to be in church on Sunday because that's what the Man upstairs wants; however, if they're not, I also know that they benefited by being raised by a man who took the time to teach them right from wrong, and for the most part could actually say, "Do what I do, as well as what I say." I will be forever grateful that church became a part of their lives before they left home because they did see the difference that a relationship with God could make. They are aware of what God can and will do in their lives. After all He's the one man who loves them more than Ron.

R
RULES

Kids want rules. They want limits. Adults are supposed to be smart enough to make rules and set boundaries and then kids know where their safe zone is and how far they can go. I don't care what kids say, they want someone to tell them what to do because it shows someone cares about them.

In my seventh and eighth grade classes, I have students who say, "I can do whatever I want. My mom doesn't care what I do." And for whatever reason, maybe she's too tired, maybe she's a single parent, or maybe no one ever cared about her, but the truth is this parent doesn't seem to care. That's why kids act up because they want to be noticed. They want someone to care enough to make rules and take the time to enforce them.

Usually when I have a student who is constantly in trouble (and I know many authorities won't agree with me) it's the parents' fault. Many times parents have told me, "We've taken away all his privileges. He's grounded until he graduates." Parents cannot just bellow out orders without making sure that they are followed. The easy part is making the rules; the difficult part is seeing that they are followed.

It's very difficult to see that a child stays off the phone when you don't want to stay home to watch him. I know in my heart that these parents have every intention of seeing that the punishment is enforced and sometimes it just sounds good to tell teachers how tough they can be. But the reality is both the kids and the teachers know that punishment will be forgotten or else just added on to, but it will never really be enforced because the parents don't want to take the time to see that it is enforced.

Now, not all parents fall into this category, but it's easy to tell which ones do. Some kids are just "bad seeds," but I truly believe those situations are very rare. The point is that kids need to know

that there are consequences to all rules, and then it's their decisions whether they break the rules or not. But, when they break the rules they must know that YOU will see that the consequences follow. If children learn at an early age that they can easily "talk you out of"" the punishment, then it won't matter if they get caught or not because they know they can get out of the punishment.

Ron was usually the enforcer. I hate to admit it, but it was easy for the kids to sweet-talk me into things. Today,

Early Wistrom Family picture   that's a problem I have as a teacher. The students know that I really don't like to punish them because I do feel sorry for them. They know it and I know it, so we deal with it.

At home, however, our rules were enforced because the boys knew that Ron would definitely make sure they knew and received the consequences.

When the boys were small I often thought Ron was too strict with them. And we often discussed it, in private. I thought that since I was in education and had taken so many classes on child behavior that I knew what would work best for the boys. However, father really did know best. I do HATE to admit that. I don't know how he learned to always do the right thing, but he did. Now again, don't assume that he was a slave driver, although the boys might say he was. All kidding aside, we weren't strict about their rooms being clean or having boys over all the time. They were involved in everything, and our house was always filled with messy little boys.

Ron was concerned with seeing that the boys knew right from wrong concerning schoolwork, dealing with others, and respecting authority. Their rules concerned safety, responsibility, respect, and logic. Looking back, it doesn't seem as if we really had many rules because the boys learned that he meant what he said, and he said what he meant. Honestly, the boys were never in trouble at school because they knew if they got trouble at school, they got in trouble at home. Remember, that's the way it used to be. It didn't matter if the teacher was right or wrong, the teacher was an adult, and adults, whether they deserve it or not, were to be respected. Disrespect was never tolerated at our home.

There was never any question about grades. The boys were never paid for good grades, which really ticked them off because they made better grades than a lot of their friends. They knew they were expected to do the best they could do. If they could look Ron in the eyes and say, "Dad, a C was the best I could do," then a C would have been acceptable; however, by the time they were in second grade, they just wouldn't lie to us. So they made As and Bs, and occasionally the Bs were questioned. We knew what the kids were capable of doing, and that's what we expected of them, to do the best with what they had.

When Grant was in third grade, we were called in for a quarterly conference. He had excellent grades except for a C in spelling. They continued to say what a precious little boy he was. They also reminded us that Grant was in the gifted program, and as a gifted child he might be bored with such menial tasks as memorizing spelling words. A student of Grant's intelligence needed to be motivated.

At that point, I wished I had not insisted that Ron accompany me to the conference ,as I knew exactly what he was thinking, and I also knew he would not keep his thoughts to himself. He proceeded, as I knew he would, to tell three teachers and two counselors that if it was motivation Grant needed then he'd certainly get it! Of course their eyes got big, and they begin to fidget and assure Ron that they all needed to agree on the motivation that would work best with Grant. And again, Ron reminded them that as

Grant's father, he knew exactly what motivation would work the best! As a fellow teacher, I was embarrassed at the thoughts I knew were going through everyone's head about Grant's dad. But, I have to admit that, in most cases, fear of being physically hurt is far more beneficial than threats of being grounded.

We left the conference, and I'm sure that everyone believed they had just set the stage for some kind of child abuse. Actually, Ron went home and discussed the situation with Grant, and guess what? Suddenly Grant realized the importance of learning his spelling words, and despite what everyone at school probably thought, Ron didn't lay one finger on Grant because he didn't have to. By that time in Grant's life, he knew when his dad said something he'd better do it. Ron did believe that sparing the rod spoiled the child, but I don't believe Ron ever spanked any of the boys past their 8th birthday. Once they learned that if they broke the rules, they had to pay the consequences, then we never had a great deal of trouble. Even today, the boys very seldom question their dad.

If parents make the rules, they have to make sure that there are consequences for the rules. Parents must make sure the rules and consequences are enforced. Making the rules is the easy part; enforcing them is far more difficult!

S
SPOILED

There are people who would say our boys were spoiled. We never made them get a job. We paid their car insurance, gave them spending money, and we usually let them sleep as late as they wanted. Now there were several reasons for this; some of of which were selfish on my part.

When they were asleep they weren't messing-up the house. Also, if they slept late, then I only had two "big" meals to fix. Our boys were never much on sandwiches or snacks, so when I say "meals," I mean MEALS. They all loved breakfast, so if they didn't wake-up until 11:00 a.m. then I would make waffles. They would have a sandwich or snack around 3:00, and we would have a big meal around 7:30 p.m. I also honestly believe that children have such a short time to be children, sleep late, and be free of responsibilities, that I wanted them to have those times as long as possible.

We also paid their car insurance until they were on their own. As long as the boys made good grades, never got into any BIG trouble, worked to their full potential at school and on the field, and loved and respected their family then we never asked them to get a job or pay their own expenses. Again we had selfish motives. If we controlled their money, we also had better control over what they could or could not do. And honestly I don't remember giving the boys a lot of money to spend. They and their friends hung-out at each other's houses, and they usually had girlfriends who seemed to be happy watching rented movies or doing other inexpensive things.

As far as cars were concerned, we bought a 1972 Bronco when we move back to Missouri. Chance and Ron restored it and Chance drove it. Then Grant and Tracey drove it until they graduated from high school. Personally, I don't think it's a good idea to buy a car for a child as soon as he turns 16, and we certainly wouldnot have bought them a new car. Again, if we own the car, and we pay the insurance, and we buy the gas, then WE have control of the car. And if a child has a job, he may buy a car, and in a sense, it's out of the parents' control, especially if he is buying his own car. It's very easy for a young person to say, "Hey, I'm paying for my car, so I can drive it whenever I want."

I would like to believe that a flashy car wouldn't have helped our boys be liked or do better in life. I always tried to tell them that people shouldn't judge you by what you drive or what you wear. Of course, the Bronco was a sharp car to drive, but the boys worked with Ron to fix it up. So in a way, they did earn it as if they had jobs. Tracey did mention that he would like to have another car to drive. Ron told him that he'd be glad to work with him to restore one like they had done to the old Bronco; however, Trace decided he didn't want to work that hard, so he'd be happy driving the Bronco or my Mazda. I can honestly say that I don't think driving a 25-year old car hurt the boys in any way.

When the boys got their scholarships we bought them each a car, not a new one, but a sharp one that looked great but had little speed. When they graduated from college, each boy had his car to trade in.

Tracey with his Bronco

As far as having jobs, we told them our job was to support them, and their jobs were to be successful students and athletes. If they fulfilled their obligations as children, then we would fulfill ours as parents. We felt that the boys' jobs centered on school and athletics.

Some people say having a job teaches responsibility. Ron and I always felt that making good grades and balancing school and sports taught them about responsibilities. And the boys always had something to do for their dad whether it was cleaning the garage, mowing the yard, or other chores.

Grant did get a job when he was 16 because he said he would rather work for someone other than his dad! The boys always said that working for Ron was much harder than working for someone else. Looking back, I'm sure it would have been much easier for me if they would have worked. There would have been less clutter around the house, fewer meals to fix, and they would have had their own spending money. But would they have gotten college scholarships or would they have been more responsible? I don't know. I only know it worked for us.

I know there are cases where kids have to work to help the family, but if your son or daughter doesn't have to work then I would not make them choose between being at summer weight lifting sessions for the football team and working at McDonalds.

Despite what anyone says, I believe being committed to a team builds responsibility and leadership more than a $5.00 an hour job!

T
THANKS

When Trace graduated from high school, I sent a letter to our local paper thanking the community for helping us raise our children. I mentioned that I didn't quote Hilary Clinton very often, but I did agree with her statement that it, "takes a village to raise a child." I would be very remiss if I didn't mention many of the people who have helped us raise three successful young men.

Ron's side of the family

So here goes. Thanks to:

Small towns where everyone knows everything about everyone and likes them inspite of it.

Teachers who still care enough to attend Little Leagues games of their students or bring watermelon on game days.

Administrators who drive school buses and know everyone by name.

Coaches who know that what works with one child doesn't

work with another child

Little town newspapers that still have articles that begin, "Well, we have to thank the Good Lord for another glorious Sunday."

Aunts who are great cooks so they let you bring the relish tray for holiday dinners.

Friends who bake cookies when the boys come home and bring peanut butter balls at Christmas.

Neighbors who watch your house when you're gone out of town to football games.

Sisters who remember birthdays.

Principals who plan Senior Citizen Proms.

Fellow teachers who cover for you when you have to leave early for another, "once in a lifetime" event.

Fans who support their teams.

Kathy's side of the family

Businesses that paint their windows with Webb City Cardinals.

New friends who treat you like old friends.

Thanks to Gammies and Grandpas.

Thanks to brothers and sisters who love your kids as much as they love their own.

Colleges like CMSU and Nebraska for giving us so many memories.

Thanks to everyone who helped our boys reach many of their goals. I could go on and on thanking everyone who's been involved in our lives.

Since this is a book about what parents might do with their children, I can only tell you that where you live and where your children go to school will have a big impact on their lives, either good or bad. Webb City was great for our boys. CMSU was the perfect choice for Chance, and Nebraska has certainly been good to Grant and Trace. I don't know if these places would be right for you, but Ron and I will always be grateful for the parts they have played in our lives.

U

UNIVERSITY OF NEBRASKA

If a boy loves football, there is truly, no place like Nebraska! When Grant was a high school senior, he was recruited by most major colleges from Stanford to Miami. After visiting Michigan, he was convinced he wanted to be a Wolverine. Michigan was in the top 10 rankings, and it looked as if they would be in the hunt for the championship title. Grant came back from his visit ready to sign.

We didn't get to go to Michigan, so we didn't know what Grant had seen or done. First rule of recruiting: If there's any way that either parent can go on the trip, then you should. Whether your athlete child thinks so or not, parents do seem to see past the cheerleaders, coeds, and the weight room. Since we couldn't go, the coaches came to see us, and it was a first class organization.

Grant and Tracey with a young Nebraska Fan

But we encouraged Grant to take the rest of his trips. Frankly, we had always been big Oklahoma fans, but OU was in a slump and Nebraska was right at the top. So Grant visited Big Red country. While in Nebraska, Trev Alberts was his guide. Trev was the top player on the team then, and he did a great job of showing Grant around. However, when Grant came home he was still sold on Michigan.

I didn't know much about Tom Osborne, but according to Ron he was an icon in college football. Coach Osborne and Ron Brown came down to visit us. I must admit that Coach Osborne was and is a very impressive figure. With his major in psychology, he's a master at remembering names and information, and to this day he always asks about Chance and my arthritis! While we wanted Grant's decision to truly be, "his decision," Ron felt that he just wasn't giving Nebraska a fair shake.

So Ron called Ron Brown and asked if Grant could make another visit to Nebraska. We would pay for the trip because it's against NCAA regulations for a school to pay for more than one visit. Of course Coach Brown thought it was a great idea. This

time Ron suggested that Grant would enjoy being with some of the players whom he would be playing with if he went to NU.

Again we went with Grant, and the rest is history. After being with some of the players, he returned to the motel room and said he wanted to be a Husker! He said he felt as if he really fit in with them. They were more like he than the Hurricanes or Wolverines. We told him not to make a snap decision, but to go home and think about it. And one morning

Grant in his first year at Nebraska

Grant said he had prayed about where to go, and when he got up in the morning, he knew he was supposed to be a Husker. Ah, the power of prayer!

God does have a plan for our lives because I can't imagine that Grant could have been any happier anywhere else! First of all, the atmosphere around Nebraska football is hard to describe. I'm sure other colleges have it, but I can't imagine anything more awe-inspiring than the sea of red that comes from all directions pouring into the stadium Saturday! Sitting in the stands, it's difficult to see any other colors.

Media Day at Nebraska

Now I realize I've been going to Nebraska games during their championship years. But, since they have had sell outs for the last 250-plus home games, I have to assume that the fans support them during thick and thin. I didn't say they didn't criticize the team or coaches, I said they attended the games! And they stay until the fat lady sings. I don't care if the score in 60-10 or if they're losing, the fans stay.

They gather for the tunnel walk in hopes their favorite player will brush their little boy's hand, and they hang around after the game to gather autographs. I'm not sure that it's really normal for people to be so crazy about football, but they love the game and they love the players. It's probably not really healthy for young men to be so adored at such an early age, but they are. Truthfully, it's probably difficult for some players to return to a normal life after being worshiped for four years! Other than that, there aren't many negatives about Husker football.

People were thrilled when Grant chose to stay for his senior year. The decision was probably selfish on Grant's part because he wasn't ready to give up the rush he felt when he ran onto the field. He was only 19, but he realized that he would never be in that time and place again, and it was something magical that could never be bought with a signing bonus.

After starting with the Rams, Grant even commented that running out under the lights for Monday Night Football didn't compare with running through the tunnel onto the field as 76,000 people hollered, "Go Big Red." Grant was fortunate that he didn't have a family depending on him, and he had the luxury of saying that money wasn't that important in his life. I will say that he's learned to adjust to it! But staying at Nebraska is a decision I'm sure he has never regretted.

The memories the boys have are something they will have for-

Grant (second from right) and other Blackshirts invite Kendell Chalmers (next to Grant)as an Honorary Blackshirt

ever. They've made lifelong friends, and while there will always be negative comments about football players, most of the young men who we have met are just down-to-earth good kids. They're polite, respectful, and they're having a great time playing a game they love. They've been coached by men like Ron Brown, who "talks the talk and walks the walk"; Tony Samuels, who helped Grant realize the player he could be; and, Charlie McBride, who made the Blackshirts believe in themselves.

During Grant's freshman year, Tracey questioned Grant about how Tom Osborne coached. Tracey kept asking him what it was that Osborne said or did that made the players so intense about playing. Tracey had been coached by many different personalities, and he was curious about Coach O's success, what he did, what he said. Grant couldn't give Tracey a pat answer. After Tracey's continuous insistence, Grant

Grant (right) gives Tracey advice at Nebraska

became frustrated and said, "Look, Tracey, I don't know what it is about him. I just know that you don't want the man to be disappointed in you. And you REALLY don't want to be called into his office."

Tracey asked Grant if he yelled or cussed, and Grant answered, "No, but when he says, 'Dag gum it' you know you are in big trouble!" That has always been one of my favorite expressions, and I am glad to know that Mr. Football, himself, uses it!

And what about our memories? We were very fortunate that one of the player's parents, the Vrzal's, felt sorry for Grant and took him into their home on holidays because his home was so far away. They, as well as their friends, the Lammers have become part of a wonderful eight-year stay in Lincoln. It's as if our boys have grown up with them, and we have all shared the highs and lows of college football.

Now that the Vrzal's son has graduated, they still tailgate and travel to the games. So does everyone else! The people who have become such a part of our lives didn't even have sons on the team, but they all share in the Nebraska mystique.

Some of the friends I've made are some "girls" (my age), who saw Grant after one of his first games walking over to us in the parking lot. They approached us and asked if they could adopt him

Ron and Kathy (left) with Nancy and Terry Vrzal

as their "special" player. It seems they always liked to have a player to cheer for and their last one had graduated. They said it made
watching the games far more fun if they knew someone on the
team.

So they cheered for Grant, and then they adopted Tracey. They,
too, have become a part of our extended family. When Grant had
his own Beanie Baby come out, one of their friends, who also feels

"Crazy Ladies" and their fellow Husker fans

that she knows the boys, made an 87 Beenie Baby for Tracey! It's a one of a kind! I call them the "Crazy Ladies."

Actually, it will probably be more difficult for us to make that last tunnel walk on Senior Day than it will be for Tracey. That's the trouble with being old. When you're young, you're excited about what the future will bring. When you're old, you know how great the past has been!

V
VISITS

Having had three boys go through the college recruiting process, I think I can offer some advice and suggestions. I know that we were better prepared by the time Tracey was recruited because we had been through it with Chance and Grant.

We moved back to Webb City during Chance's junior year of high school. He only had one season to play football and be noticed by college coaches in the midwest. Ron and I are extremely grateful to Coach Jerry Kill, who was Chance's high school football coach, for guiding both Chance and us through the football season. Being a small town, most of the Webb City players had been together since youth football. Many coaches would have been hesitant to give Chance a fair shake; however, Coach Kill played a dominant role in helping Chance achieve his dream of playing college ball.

Chance had a great senior year. But, since he hadn't been in Webb City very long, many colleges who had been watching Webb City through the years did not know much about the new Wistrom kid. Coach Kill took it upon himself to find colleges where Chance would be able to make a contribution on the field. Chance heard from many Division II schools because most Division I schools thought he was too small to play defensive end. Even some D II school shared that thought; however, Coach Kill knew that Chance could and would be able to contribute right away. Thus the recruiting process began!

Tip # 1. Always fill out all information and return it to the college recruiter. Maybe it's not your first choice. Maybe you think you're Division I material because you were named First Team All Conference. Guess what? There are a lot of young men who feel the same as you, and colleges only have so many scholarships to offer. If those scholarships are taken by the time you decide, then you may be sorry you didn't return that postcard.

Tip # 2. Always be polite and respectful to anyone who calls or visits. Again, maybe you're thinking, "No way, Jose" would I go there! But, you never know what the future holds for you, so don't close any doors. Besides, coaching is a fellowship, and it doesn't hurt to have coaches from other teams saying good things about you.

And while you're at it, respect and courtesy are things that we never outgrow. I always tell my students to say, "Yes, sir," and "Thank you." Courtesy is something very uncommon today, and adults notice it and will remember you for it. When Chance was being recruited, some of the coaches even asked some of the merchants about his behavior. It doesn't hurt to be kind and considerate to people because you never know who knows whom. Just remember the Golden Rule. It works.

Tip # 3. Show your intelligence. Use common sense. The number of scholarships being offered is less than ever, so schools have to be very careful about whom they recruit. I really believe that the time has passed where coaches can ignore a young man's behavior or grades. Oh, I know there are circumstances when a player may be so dynamic that a staff may look the other way when they hear stories about him, but, I don't believe that's true for most recruits. Coaches have to consider all areas of a young man's life, and if two players are equal on the field than what they do off the field will be judged. The player with the better reputation in and out of the classroom will be offered the scholarship. Ron used to tell the boys that they weren't Deion Sanders, so they better have something else going for them.

Tip # 4. I know kids won't want to hear this, but they should take their parents, not a girlfriend, on their recruiting visit. As I said before, parents may notice something that players won't. We also had coaches tell us that they hated to see a girl hanging all over a recruit because that usually meant the young man might have trouble adjusting to college life. According to the coach, he could handle a young man who was homesick, but he couldn't compete with a cute little blonde! So, boys leave your date at home!

Tip # 5. Dress like you are going to a decent restaurant. You don't need to wear a coat and tie, but Do NOT wear baggy pants with your underwear showing. If you have to wear a hat, remove it when you go inside. Don't sit there slouched in a chair with your hat on backward and a toothpick in your mouth. Now you may think this sounds like common sense, but I have seen kids dressed this way on recruiting trips. I don't know where their mamas were when they left the house, but she should have been checking their suitcases!

Tip # 6. Remember, as Aretha Franklin said, "R-E-S-P-E-C-T" is the key word. The college and the coaches you are visiting have spent a lot of time and money to bring you to them. Show them the respect they deserve. Stand up when they walk over to greet you; answer them with complete answers, not "Yea" and "huh." Look them in the eye when they speak, and listen to what they say. Act enthusiastic. Let them know that at this moment in time you can't imagine any other place you would rather be than right there talking about football. You may think you are God's gift to football, but don't act like it!

Tip # 7. Don't embarrass yourself or your school. Don't do anything stupid just because you're away from home. Go to the activities that the school has planned for you whether it's something you want to do or not. Again, they've gone to a lot of trouble for you, so appreciate it and enjoy it. You are a high school student, so don't try and impress anyone by trying to act like a college man. Don't try to practice COOL. Worry about being cool after you've signed on the dotted line. Better yet, wait until your first few weeks of two-a-days, and then see how "cool" you really feel.

Tip # 8. Take most, if not all of your visits. You're bound to be impressed with the first place you go because it is an exciting experience. But you may be like Grant and find out that the first place wasn't really right for you after all. I do think it's wrong to continue the visits once you've made-up your mind for sure, because it takes time and money to sponsor a visit. But be sure before you make a commitment. We met one young man who had told every college that he visited that he was going to THAT college. Coach Larry Smith from the University of Missouri called Grant as one of his first recruits when he was hired. Grant really liked Coach Smith and he felt he would have been a great coach. By then, however, Grant had decided to go to Nebraska, so he didn't think it was fair to take a visit to Missouri, especially since it was so late in the recruiting process. I think Coach Smith appreciated his honesty. I'm not sure if other Missouri fans did.

Tip # 9. Spend some time researching the school. Know what's important for you and make a list of your questions. If it's important to be close to home, then keep that as a high priority. If it's important that you play then make sure you find a school where you know you will have a chance to be on the field. If playing time is important to you, then you may want to look at a smaller college instead of the largest one interested in you. You're still getting an education. Don't let others influence you. Listen to their advice and suggestions, but just because someone else thinks it's a great place doesn't mean you will.

Tip # 10. Enjoy yourself. Realize the opportunity that awaits you. Don't be afraid to step out of your comfort zone. Weigh your options, prioritize, ask for advice, and when all else fails, pray about it. Ultimately, this does have to be your decision because it will be four or five years out of your life. You'd better make sure that you're going to be happy there!!!

Parents, my advice to you is to be there for your child. If possible, go on the recruiting visits. Offer suggestions whether they are solicited or not. You, as a parent, also have an obligation to the colleges and coaches. You need to make sure that forms are filled out and returned. Even if you think your child REALLY is too talented for that football program, each school deserves the same attention and respect.

I always thought it would be a good thing to send a thank you note to the coach. Of course that was one of my "good ideas" that I didn't follow through with, but I still think it would have been a nice thing to do.

W
WOMEN

Our boys were raised to respect women. I will say that they are somewhat chauvinistic, and that's probably my fault. I truly believe that a mother's place is to be at home when her children are at home. Teaching allowed me to do this. Until the boys were old enough so that they were gone a lot, I was never very involved in activities unless my children were involved.

Like most women, I did, at times, resent all the time I spent at home being Super Mom. I wanted to have time to myself, and I honestly think all women need that. I was never able to convince anyone else about that theory. My teaching job was 7:30 to 4:00, and then my other job was 4:00 to whenever . All of the boys hated to come into an empty house. I won't say I had chocolate chip cookies waiting when they came in the door, but I was there for them and their friends. Luckily, I had two good friends, Anne and Nona, who took care of the cookies.

Kathy and Nona Spence

There are so many career-oriented women today, and I understand the reasons, but before young people get married they need to think about who or what their priorities are and where their commitments lie. Too many babies are having babies, getting divorced, and no one is thinking about the children. I believe my boys appreciate what I did, and I think they will want their children to be raised the same way if it's economically possible.

Today's women recognize the need to develop a life beyond

being a mother, but in the long run may forget what Cosmo says, children deserve a full-time mother. And if you can be one, then you should. My job was to be a mother first.

Besides being a mother, I am also a woman, and I've talked to the boys about the way women feel and how they want to be treated. But, it's time someone told young women how they should treat young men. As a teacher I have never found a note with sexual comments written by a young man, but I have found several sexually explicit notes with graphic details written by little girls. Young ladies don't write notes explaining what they would like done to them, they don't call boys offering them gifts; they don't walk into a pizza place and grope a football player.

We've tried to teach our boys to respect women, to remember that every young woman is someone's daughter or sister. We have told them that "NO" means "NO" regardless of what has transpired up until that point. We have also told them that there are a lot of unhappy young women who would do anything to be a part of someone's life.

I know many people will find what I'm writing as very offensive, but we need to look at what is happening to both men and women in today's society. If young men are different than they were 20 years ago, then young women are different also. The moral values have changed drastically, and while many people might say I'm biased having raised three boys, I honestly think that women have changed more.

Fair or not, women have always been responsible for drawing the lines and making the rules. Today there are not any lines and few rules, or else women change them in the middle of the game. There are so many confused families with confused children, and it doesn't seem to be getting any better. Boys think they can do whatever they want to prove they are men, and then walk away from their responsibilities because they've seen their friends or even fathers do the same. Young women who are insecure about themselves will do anything for anyone who says they love them.

Babies are just the spoils of war. Children need guidelines, and it's time that parents became more responsible for showing their children what is acceptable behavior. But please don't blame only

Dee and Chance

young men. The young women who pursue them must also be held accountable.

As parents we have to teach our young men how to treat young ladies, and we must teach our young women how to be young ladies. Between MTV and the movies, young people think that anything goes. While my boys did watch that stuff, we also told them that just because it was on TV didn't make it acceptable behavior. Just because there are no morals on TV anymore does not mean that the greatest director of all rewrote the script.

If parents aren't going to teach their children how to be young ladies and gentlemen, then they should be willing to let others take charge. I am amazed at the parents who never come to school when their children are making Fs, but as soon as we try to impose our "morals" on these children, the parents come flying up to school and protest that "you can tell my baby how to act." That's not part of your job." But it is everyone's job when no one wants to be held accountable.

As the mother of three boys, I do become very defensive about this topic because I know that while young men are not always perfect, young women also get carried away with their behavior. Yet it's the young men who are always held accountable. Lives can be ruined by a broken heart, and often the truth isn't nearly as sensational as the half-truths that have been written.

X
EXTRA

Even if the boys wouldn't have played college ball, our lives have been filled with what I call "Kodak Moments." Those are the moments that you never want to forget. I could go on and on about those times and memories, but many would probably be a lot like your memories. Instead, this chapter will talk about those "X-TRA" football events, some good and some bad, that have happened to us as we traveled from Florida to California.

Webb City High School Football

All of the boys finished their high school careers in Webb City, Missouri. To me there is nothing to compare with a high school football game, especially in a small town like Webb City. When high school players get on the field, you know they are playing with heart and soul. They're not playing because they have a scholarship or contract. They're playing because they love the game.

Many of the young men will never play past the high school level. Their only reward will come when they hear the crowd cheer. And if fortunate enough, they'll be recognized if they win a state championship. To some young men, Friday night football is the height of their high school career. This may sound dorky, but I think the first state title Grant's team won was probably just as exciting as his college championship or the Super Bowl.

Now, I know you do think I'm crazy, but watching the highlight tape of Grant's high school championship team gives me goose bumps! I can't explain it, but it's a thrill I'll never forget, and neither will the players. The entire town showed up for a parade. We had autograph-signing session for the team, and everywhere the players went they were idolized.

Grant, Ron, Kathy, Supt. Dr. Lankford at Webb City's Grant Wistrom Day

Our little town could be a postcard for Andy Griffith's Mayberry. Friday night football games are the social events of the season. All generations come to cheer their children, grandchildren, or someone else's. People begin lining up at the ticket gates as early as 1:30 p.m. if it's supposed to be a good game. When Grant was playing, there was an older couple, Don and Ann Witherspoon, who would pack dinner and take chairs to sit and play cards while they waited for tickets, and they didn't even have any relatives playing.

When the gates are opened everyone runs to throw down their blankets to guarantee the best seats. Everyone from babies to senior citizens wear red with the school mascot, a Cardinal, somewhere on them. You can imagine the thrill those young football players feel when they walk out onto the field at 6:00 p.m. and the stands are already filled to capacity. I know it certainly must be intimidating to the opposing team!

These same fans will travel as far as the games will take them, and like the mailman they won't let rain, sleet, snow, or hail (or anything else) deter them on their mission to cheer the Cardinals on to victory. Car windows, as well as businesses, are decorated with cheers and Cardinal drawings! Following a spontaneous prayer, the cheerleaders get the fans to their feet, and in some cases the fans remain standing most of the game. The fall air is crisp and cool, and when you hear your son's name called over the loud speaker there isn't anything to compare with it! And I will say it again, THERE IS NOTHING THAT CAN COMPARE TO A FRIDAY NIGHT HIGH SCHOOL FOOTBALL GAME. If your community does not support youth sports, then you probably need to move!

Central Missouri State Universtiy Football

Chance played at Webb City his senior year only. They lost in the first round of the playoffs, and I can still remember how devastated he was when they lost. Chance, as well as Grant and Tracey, believe that there is no other place other than first. I never understood how much a winning attitude had to do with making someone a good player until I listened to college coaches talk about a winning mentality. If losing is unacceptable, and winning is the only option, then a player or coach will work more and harder than other players who are used to losing. I know that no one wants to lose, but if it gets to the point that it no longer bothers a player to lose, then gradually losing may become acceptable behavior. With young players, a coach has to teach players to put the game behind them, but a coach must also be able to build that desire to win in his players.

Although Chance's team didn't win a state championship, he was named a second team All-American, and thus the recruiting process began. Coaches have always questioned the size of all of the boys. They wondered if they were big enough to play college ball. Chance's coach, Jerry Kill, knew that Chance was playing defensive end at 165 pounds, but he knew Chance had the heart and determination of a much bigger player.

While Chance was overlooked by Division I schools, many

Division II colleges recruited him. Being new to the recruiting scene we didn't know what to expect. Nevertheless, it was an exciting time for us; having college coaches come to the house; visiting colleges; waving to Chance as he flew off to Warrensburg in the plane they had sent for him. After making several visits,

Chance at CMSU

Chance decided on Central Missouri State.

When Chance began playing college football, it was all new to us. Grant and Tracey were still playing in Webb City, but we would load the car on Saturday and drive to Warrensburg, Missouri to watch the Mules! Ron still remarks that those days were his favorite: Thursday nights with Tracey in junior high football; Fridays with Grant at the high school; and, Saturday with Chance at the Burg.

We would usually stay in Warrensburg Saturday night, and Chance and his friends would ask us to hang out with them. We became friends with several of the parents, and we would go to the local places downtown after the games. Looking back, it was a perfect time for us. We thoroughly enjoyed Chance's friends, and they always seemed to enjoy having us around. The boys always liked talking to Ron because he would say exactly what he thought about their playing both on and "off" the field. To this day, Chance's friends always ask about us, and we try to keep up with them. While Warrensburg isn't a Nebraska, it's a great school. Chance got a wonderful education, made some great friends, and found a perfect wife for him. What more could you want?

Nebraska Fans

The only thing that surpasses a Webb City football game is one at Nebraska. As I said in the Nebraska chapter, there is nothing like being a part of the Big Red Machine. They love their football players, and they show it in everything they do.

One of the neatest things at Nebraska is the tunnel walk. The boys come out of the locker room and walk through a roped area that takes them out onto the field. Fans line the ropes to shout cheers at their favorite players. Parents hold up their children so that they can slap hands with a 300-pound lineman. After the game, they wait there hoping to get a signature on a program or football.

Grant was always very good about signing things although, one day I had the most bizarre request ever made of me. After a game, Ron and I were waiting for Grant. A young lady came flying up to our car dragging two little children

Kathy and other Nebraska fans in San Diego

behind her. She wanted to know if we were Grant's parents and if we were waiting for him. Then she began to tell us this story about how Grant was her favorite player, and what she loved most about him was his stomach. Then she showed us pictures where she had shaved his number in her head.

When Grant came out she asked if he would have his picture taken with her and her two children. He agreed, and I took the picture. Then she asked me, since I was his mother, if I would take a picture of her kissing his stomach. Grant looked at me with big puppy dog eyes begging me to do something about it. But honestly, not having ever been asked this before, I didn't know what to say, other than, "OK." Boy, did I hear about it from Grant and Ron. Grant said he couldn't believe that his own mother would let a strange woman kiss his stomach and then take a picture of her doing it. I tried to explain, but Grant kept saying he felt "so violated." Several weeks later I got a very nice letter from the young woman, and she wasn't a groupie or a stalker, just a fan.

We always joke that one day we might see that picture in the *Enquirer*!

Basketball Titles

While we are obviously huge football fans, my favorite sport is basketball. I loved watching Tracey play basketball. In basketball, you're so close to the court that you can see the players' faces and at times read their lips. Sometimes that's a good thing, and sometimes it's not! When Tracey and his friends played it was as if they knew what each other was thinking. They worked together like a well-oiled machine.

When Trace was a junior, one of his best friends, Shawn, was a senior but a lot smaller than Trace. Shawn moved all over the court like a water bug. He was also more verbal on the court. The other team's players would often try to fluster Trace by saying things about Grant or comparing Trace to Grant. Tracey wouldn't say a word, but Shawn always had something to say back to them. Shawn never got caught, but it looked like Samson taking up for Goliath.

The following year when Trace was a senior, his football team lost in the second round of state playoffs. I don't think any of the players have ever forgotten how they felt. The entire team was such a good bunch of kids; no hot shots, big super stars, just some quiet hard working young men who had planned their senior year around winning a state football championship.

Neither Tracey nor any of his friends ever commented very

much on the loss, but when Trace's basketball team made it to the state playoffs, I know he didn't want to have a repeat of the football game. Watching the tapes of the championship game, you can see the determination in Tracey's eyes. For 48 minutes the entire team never let up. Players stepped up and made plays they hadn't made before. There were no ball hogs or hot shots, just a group of boys who really understood the meaning of teamwork.

As they piled all over each other after the final buzzer, the crowd went wild. Personally, I was estatic for Coach Johnson because he was so happy for his boys. As I watched them celebrate, I thought how all children should be able to experience at

Tracey, coach Johnson, Grant
after basketball championship

least "one moment in time" where everyone is cheering for them. Everyone should have the opportunity to be someone's hero.

Another Michael Jordan?

Chance didn't play basketball, but Grant did, or rather he tried. Where Tracey looked as if he could glide through the air, Grant looked like a plough horse clomping down the court. Chance knew he looked the same way, but he was smart enough to stay off the court! Grant was basically a big body put out there to block the lane. He wasn't really allowed to dribble the ball or run with it, and if Grant hadn't fouled out by half time we considered he was having a good game. Once he stole the ball, and dribbled down the court. (I use the work "dribble" cautiously, but I'm not sure what else to call it.) He was going up for a slam dunk, and the crowd rose to its feet. Grant went up, slammed the ball, came down and watched the ball bounce out of the basket. His shoulders drooped, his head dropped to his chest, and the crowd loved it!

When Nebraska was recruiting Grant, Coach Osborne flew down to see him. While Osborne couldn't actually talk to Grant (NCAA rule) he could watch him. In this case he watched him play basketball. It was the game where Grant had four fouls in the first four minutes, so he didn't play again until the second half. Within two minutes he had fouled out! Coach Osborne had flown down from Nebraska to watch Grant sit on the bench. Later T.O. told Ron that it was obvious that Nebraska wasn't recruiting Grant for basketball!

National Championship, Nebraska Style

The year that Grant decided to go to Nebraska, we watched Nebraska lose a national title to Florida State. Everyone said that

Grant at Nebraska

Coach Osborne couldn't win the Big One. He certainly proved that those critics were wrong!

While Grant was at Nebraska they won three national titles. And we had a great time watching them do it. The Orange Bowl was finally good to Nebraska! We would take off either before or after Christmas to spend several days with the team. As usual, the Nebraska faithful followed. Terrorists could take over the state, and no one would notice until the Bowl Game ended! Our friends from Nebraska would meet us there, and while the boys had to practice and follow curfew, we would have a great time!!

During Grant's last year, it was questionable if the Huskers could win the title. Michigan was ranked ahead of them, and it would all come down to the team's bowl game performances. Since it wasn't known until the last minute that Nebraska would play in the Orange Bowl, hotel rooms were hard to find. I had gotten on the Internet and found what I thought was a great deal! A quaint two-room cottage on Miami Beach, it sounded like a great place. While our little Nebraska group usually stayed together, this time most of the other Nebraska fans were coming at different times and staying at different places. I was very pleased at what I had found, and I assured Ron that the pictures looked great.

We arrived late in the evening, and I was glad, because if Ron had seen it in the daylight, I'm sure he would have left, and perhaps left me. Personally, I liked it. It had a Bohemian atmosphere about it, like somewhere a couple bicycling across Europe might stay. OK, it wasn't the Ritz, it wasn't even the Holiday Inn, but it had everything it advertised; right on the beach, close to shopping, etc. Once you got used to it, it wasn't too bad. Of course the windows were broken, and the place was somewhat dirty, but if you overlooked those things it was OK. After all what could you expect for $70 a day on Miami Beach? Our friends from Webb City, Nona and Dale, came for the game, and when Nona saw it she agreed with Ron. I guess it did leave a little to be desired. I think Nona spent the morning of her arrival cleaning it. I almost had Ron convinced that it was just another adventure when the unthinkable happened.

Several agents had contacted us about representing Grant. One of the biggest agents in the country, Leigh Steinberg, had called about meeting was us in Miami. Where we were staying there was only one phone for all the guests. It was located in the patio area! When we finally got to talk to Mr. Steinberg he asked where we were staying. He said it was the only place he'd ever called where

Chance, Tracey, Grant at hotel in Miami Beach

the same person (in this case the 80-year old owner) answered the phone whether he called at 6:00 a.m., noon, or midnight! He offered to come to our hotel, but Ron assured him we would be more than happy to visit him at his hotel. Ron's still a little touchy about that one!

When we met with the young man whom they modeled the movie Jerry McGuire after, he was perfectly charming. I'm sure he would have understood if he had visited us at Kathy's Motel!

You know the rest of the story. Nebraska gave Florida such a thorough thrashing that Nebraska and Michigan shared the title. We celebrated with Grant and Jason Peter after the game. As I stood on the corner feeling like the Beverly Hillbillies watching Grant and Jason drive off in a limo to experience South Beach, I realized Grant's life would never be the same again; and it hasn't been!

The Super Bowl

That probably says it all! Of course the Super Bowl is the King of Football. However, I will admit when Grant was drafted by the Rams, Ron and I never thought that we would be watching Grant play in it after two seasons. After listening to horror stories about people leaving their Ram tickets on car windshields, who would have thought the Rams would be in the Super Bowl, much less win it!

But when we realized that they were going to Atlanta, we started making our plans! I can't speak for other teams, but I'll have to say that the Rams' organization treated us with golden gloves. Their first "gift" came when Grant told us that if we came to St. Louis, we could fly free on the Rams's charter to Atlanta. Also, each player had two hotel rooms, so we would be staying at the Hilton, again free of charge! As the world's biggest penny pincher, I was thrilled. The best part of all was that all of us - Chance, Dee, Tracey, Ron, and I - would all get to be together for the week.

I kept a diary of our week. Here are some of the entries.

January 27 (in St. Louis):

7:30 a.m. : Get up and shower. Stomach has butterflies. Read the Post-Dispatch. Disappointed there are no pictures of Grant. Wish Ron had let him play quarterback when he was Grant's coach. Papers always show the quarterbacks! I guess every mother feels that way.

9:40 a.m.: Arrive at Rams Park. Everything is so organized. I'm used to being the travel guide, but this is nice. Early, of course. With Big R, you are usually the first ones to arrive. Good thing, we had the first choice of the food!

The Rams did a fantastic job of organization. When we drove up to Rams Park, they had someone waiting to meet us and check our bags according to the hotel. Then we just sat back and watched the others arrive.

10:00 a.m.: Snacks, watch everyone come in. Little kids are everywhere. New generation. I would have left mine with Gammy and Grandpa. Watched Kurt Warner's wife. She must feel that she's living in a fairy tale. Seems very nice, sincere. Love her hair. Would love to cut mine like hers. Mentioned that to Chance and Tracey. Empathic "NO." Guess you have to be thin and young, not old and fat.

10:40 a.m.: Police escort to the airport. We ride right up to the plane. I could get used to this. No lines, no hassle, just get on the plane. Every seat has a sack lunch.

11:25 a.m.: Take-off! I hum the words to, "Georgia on My Mind" as I close my eyes and remininsce over the past year. I hope I get to meet Georgia Frontiere, the owner, and thank her. Probably won't happen, so maybe I'll send her a letter! This is going to be a great trip!

1:30 p.m.: LAND! Quickly, I try to stuff all the extra goodies in my bag. Tracey and Chance roll their eyes at me, but I notice that Dee and most of the other mothers are doing the same thing! All mothers must be alike. At 11:00 tonight, the boys won't be too embarrassed to eat those smashed sandwiches!

3:00 p.m.: Get to the hotel. It's NICE! When Grant first told us about the room, I thought we might embarrass him if all five of us stayed in one room, so I thought about getting another one so we wouldn't be so crowded. HOWEVER, when I found out the rooms were $275.00, we requested a roll-a-way bed! Grant wasn't embarrassed as he said he had lived with me too long to even consider that I would pop for another room. So we did a lot of bonding, especially since we spent so much time at the hotel since Atlanta had a major ice storm!

That night Grant came over, and we went to eat. The Rams had a fantastic dinner with shrimp and prime rib. Throughout our stay, the Rams always had someone available to help us or offer suggestions on what to do. The hospitality room was always open with snacks and Cokes. We never wanted for anything. It's a first class football team!

January 28 (in Atlanta):

ICE STORM IS STAYING IN ATLANTA! Even that couldn't dampen our spirits. The Rams had charter buses to take us wherever we wanted to go. They had shopping for the women and fun places for kids. We spent that day at the mall, which wasn't a thrill for the boys, but Dee and I had fun. That night we met Grant again for dinner as he had access to a car, although I was scared to death to be driving on the ice.

Went to a great place for dinner where many of the players were eating. As I visited with the various players who came by our table, I leaned over to Ron and whispered, "Can you believe we are sitting here with all these players we've seen on Monday Night Football?"

Ron looked at me with this look of disbelief. "You really are a blonde," he responded. "Did it ever occur to you that your son IS one of those Monday Night Football players?"

Suddenly, it hit me that, yes, he was. But, as I watched him teasing with his brothers, I thought he's still just "Boog." I hope it always stays that way.

January 29:

NFL EXPERIENCE. I guess they do this at every Super Bowl, but the NFL fills an entire convention center with games, exhibits, card shows, etc. There's something for everyone. They have a pass and kick competition for the kids. NFL coaches give talks on various subjects. There are high-tech video games for young and old. I even found something for me. I am always complaining that anyone could be a commentator for a football game as there are certain things announcers always say or ask. You can count on an, "It's gut check time," when it's third and one. Or you can expect a, "So Coach, what did you tell your players at half time to help them overcome this 21-point deficit?" Talk about a blonde question!

Anyway, the NFL Experience had it set up where two people could "pretend" to be broadcasters with headphones, microphones and a televised football game. So Dee and I became John Madden and Boomer Eiason. Your voices were broadcast throughout the area, and if I say so myself, we were a big hit! Everyone gathered around to listen to us, and it was great. I do have a better appreci-

Dee and Kathy, day commentary at NFL Experience at Super Bowl XXXIV

ation for what sports announcers do. But, I want to go on record that I never included John Madden or Keith Jackson in this group. After all John put Grant on his All-Madden team, and Jackson is a big Nebraska fan, so I certainly don't want to alienate them.

There was also a room filled with everything imaginable for collectors. I kept looking for things with Grant's name, but Ron kept telling me that I wouldn't find anything because he wasn't a high profile player. WELL, HE IS IN MY BOOK. At one point I found the cardboard figures of players. They had Kurt Warner, Peyton Manning, etc. When I asked about Grant, the guy said, "Who? Never heard of him! Who does he play for?" I was hot! So I found Dee and Chance. At different times Chance and Dee went back and asked about Grant. Dee went last and the guy told her he guessed he'd better find out who the Wistrom kid was as she was the fourth one to ask about him. I still don't know who the other one was.

That afternoon, we got together with one of Chance's good friends from Florida. Jason Varitek is now a catcher for the Boston

Red Sox, but his home is in Atlanta. It was fun to see him and listen as he and Chance discussed all the things they had done in Florida, things we knew nothing about! Remember, we had always considered Chance "the good son."

Now we realize he just didn't get caught!

After another great dinner, the kids rode the Metro to downtown Atlanta for the night scene. Needless to say, I was a wreck. I envisioned all kinds of things that could happen to them, from getting mugged to freezing to death. The song from the '60s about the man who rode "forever beneath the streets" kept going through my mind! I think Ron was worried, too, but he knew I'd worry enough for both of us. Chance and Dee got back before Trace, and as usual Chance saw the humor in the situation. He said if Tracey wasn't back by game time, he got to sell Tracey's ticket. In a short time Tracey returned, and I quizzed all of them about why they didn't call us. Considering Chance and Dee were 28, and Tracey was 21, and they had been on their own for quite a while, they just couldn't understand my concern! Every time I bring this up, Tracey reminds me that he was with Ram fans, as if that was the answer to everything. Now, whenever he's with us, he'll call to let us know where he is or if he'll be late. I don't think children ever truly understand how parents worry until they have children of their own.

January 30 - SUPER BOWL SUNDAY:

The Rams buses took everyone to the game, and it was wonderful not having to fight the traffic or the ice. Actually, the game is almost a blur because the entire memory almost seems as if it were a figment of my imagination. It's as if it never happened. The entertainment was awesome; we had great seats; but it was just surreal. Like a dream. Usually I spend more time at a game watching the cheerleaders or the people. And as I sat there wide-eyed like a little kid, Ron hugged me and said, "You really don't have a clue what you're witnessing here. Your son is playing in the biggest sporting event in the world." Then he patted my head like you do a dumb animal.

I always knew they would win. Of course, as I've said before, I always think that good things happen to good people. I'm sure that Steve McNair's mother feels the same way.

January 31:

After the game, the Rams held a huge celebration party! Wonderful food, entertainment, conversation, etc. As I looked around I realized that many of the players would either be traded or not have their contracts renewed. Wives, children, and lives would be changed forever. Homes would have to be sold, and new homes decorated. Tears would be shed over leaving old friends, and new friends would be made.

(l-r) Kathy, Ron , Chance, Grant, Dee, Tracey after Super Bowl XXXIV

Yes, this is a glamorous life style; however, like all good things, there's always a down side. I sat at a table with a woman with three small children. Her handsome husband was table-hopping as the other players were, and I watched as young women followed him and hung on his every word. I'm not sure I could have been as graceful as she was being. The NFL football life is a tough life for a young wife and mother. As much as I have enjoyed Grant's success, I only hope that he will be able to return to what I call a normal life.

When we flew back that morning, Grant got to return with us. It was so much fun watching all my "babies" review the game! It just doesn't get any better!

Famous People: They put on their pants one leg at a time...

I am always in awe of anyone who has been on TV or is well known. Ron always reminds me that they're just human; they put on their pants one leg at a time. Although I still get tongue-tied when I meet someone whom I consider to be famous, I am beginning to realize that crazy things happen to them just as they happen to us.

When Stanford was recruiting Grant, Bill Walsh visited our home in Webb City. At the time we had a dog called Meathead who was a cross between a greyhound and who knows what else. As Bill Walsh was walking up to our door, Meathead jumped up and tried to bite him on the ear. The only comment that Coach Walsh made was, "Boy that dog can really jump high!" Later we visited Coach Walsh in California, and he graciously entertained us at his house. He and his wife were charming, and Ron's right. He probably does put on his pants one leg at a time.

Another recruiter from Stanford who visited us was Keena Turner. Again, not being a huge football fan, I didn't have a clue who Keena Turner was. When Ron excitedly told me that Turner was coming to recruit Grant, I was highly impressed. After all I didn't know of many high school seniors who were being visited by TINA TURNER!

Then there was the time Chance pretended to be Bobby Bowden calling me about Grant. In his Bobby Bowden voice, he questioned me about Grant. I did fine until he started asking me why Chance didn't play Division I ball and why he wasn't as good as Grant? Well, I jumped on that with both feet telling "Bobby" that Chance Wistrom was as good as Grant and if we had been in

Tracey and Keena (Tina) Turner

Webb City longer he would have played at Nebraska also. By the time Ron got home I was in tears because I told him, "I'd made a complete fool of myself with Bobby Bowden." I even called Grant's high school coach and told him to call Bobby Bowden and explain that I'd been under a lot of pressure lately and that's why I talked so crazy! Or else tell him Grant was adopted; I wasn't his real mother. Finally Chance let me know what he had done, but everyone certainly enjoyed the joke at my expense. As word got around, I felt like I couldn't answer the phone because I never knew if it really was a Tom Osborne or a Chance Wistrom!

Y
YOUTH SPORTS

As you have read this book, you've read all the comments about coaches and parents and rules. Despite all the negative things said about youth sports, your child may fall behind if he doesn't start playing until he's in junior high. But, if he wants to play and you agree to let him, then remember it's a commitment on everyone's part. So make sure you are as committed as your son or daughter.

Remind him that once he starts, he has to finish the season. He doesn't have to play next year, but he can't quit in the middle of the year. You may even want him to quit because it will make your life easier, but don't give in. Remember, kids need to learn that quitting is not the answer to problems.

Some people will say that participating in organized sports at such an early age can cause children to get burned-out at a young age. We found that the opposite was true. The more the kids played, the better they became, and the more they wanted to play. Yes, they were good players, but that's because Ron worked with them. Many people think that Ron must have been some super athlete. The truth is he never played high school sports. He is just a father who learned what he could about the sports the boys played. He approached Pop Warner like he does everything, with complete honesty. He was fair and honest, and he studied what it was that made good football players into great football players.

Chance in third grade football

I know there are some very bad youth coaches. In some cases a poor coach can do more to hurt a kid than help one, but that's where you as a parent have to help. Don't yell at the coach, and complain about him in front of your child. If what the coach is teaching your child isn't right, and it's not working, then it might be time to talk to your child. If he's old enough, explain to him how you feel about the coach.

This is really difficult because you don't want your child to disrespect the coach, but you don't want him to learn the incorrect way

Grant as a baseball player

to hit or catch. Maybe now is the time to volunteer to help with the team. If all else fails, you may have to talk to the coach. I said talk to him, not confront him or belittle him. Just make sure that you are upset with the coach for the right reasons.

As the boys got older, Ron did discuss coaches with the boys. They talked about why they thought the coach did certain things, or what they could do to make the team a better team. But Ron never made negative remarks that would make the boys lose

respect for their coaches. He may have said things to me, but he never belittled the coach in front of the players.

If your kids want to play in youth sports, then get involved; coach, help with the field, work in the concession stand. Always go to the games. Cheer for all the kids. Enjoy yourself! This time will never come again.

Frankly, I wish we could go back to the times where everyone went to the ballpark on weeknights in the summer. Kids didn't have flashy uniforms, expensive gloves, or special cleats. No one went to summer camps, and the All Star team was saved for when you were older. It was something special; something to look forward to. Kids weren't committed to traveling teams for the entire summer. They had a chance to be kids without any pressure about who made what team and where you were going.

Now, don't get me wrong. When we were in Florida, the boys traveled all over the state playing football games. It was our social life. I loved staying in motels and eating out. But it was fun to return to Missouri where things were slower and quieter; however, eventually Missouri caught up with Florida.

I don't know what the answer is. If your kids don't play organized football, then they may get behind. If they play, they may get burned out, or even worse, they may have a terrible coach who doesn't know the fundamentals. It's a tough call, but you know your child better than anyone else, so you're the ref. You make the call.

Z
ZZZZZ - THE END

I can't really end this book. Although I'm now 53 and Ron is 55, we're both looking forward to grandchildren, more football games, and many more "once in a lifetime" thrills.

When I was younger I couldn't wait till I got older. When the boys were little I couldn't wait until they were old enough to dress themselves. Then I wanted them to be able to help each other, be left alone, start school. I was excited when they started in youth sports. I loved going to high school games. Then came college and now the NFL.

Now, I want time to stand still. I want things to slow down. I want to remember every moment of Tracey's senior year. I plan to keep a diary of his final season. Where I used to think about going shopping in Lincoln because I had tired of football, I don't want to miss a thing about this season. For those of you with young chil-

The Boys

dren, slow down, enjoy them. Start that journal about the funny things they say, or someday you'll be like me and you won't remember half of them!

It is truly amazing how God has planned the stages in our lives.

When one door closes another one opens. Just when I think it can't get any better something else happens that reminds me time marches on, and there's something better around the corner.

In case you haven't been able to tell, Ron and I feel that we were truly blessed to have been the parents of three rowdy little boys. Once I mentioned to a reporter if I had known it would be this much fun, I would have had several more. And we wish we had. I can't say the boys were perfect or they won't ever disappoint me, but then they probably can't say that about me either!

So this is the end of one chapter in our lives....

But the beginning of many more. It's been one heck of a ride!

Ron and Kathy

STELLAR PRESS ORDER FORM

Title	Unit Price	Quantity Ordered	Extended Price
How 'Bout Them Rams - A Guide To The History of Rams Football by Jim Hunstein	$19.95		
The Cardinals Chronology - A Chronological History of the St. Louis Cardinals by Tim Steele	$19.95		
Mrs. Wistrom's ABCs - What I Learned Raising Three All Americans by Kathy Sasse Wistrom	$16.95		
The Glory Years of the St. Louis Cardinals - Volume I The World Championship Seasons by Mel Freese	$19.95		
Infamous St. Louis Crimes & Mysteries by David Linzee	$19.95		
The Tooth Fairy Palace by Randi Naughton & Allex Oelkers	$9.95		
Sub-Total			
Sales Tax @ 7.225% (Missouri Residents Only)			
Shipping & Handling ($4 for first book, $2.50 ea. add'l book)			
Total Amount Due			

If you pay by credit card, you may fax this order toll free to 1-877-572-8835.

Credit Card Number: _____

Expriation Date: _____ Name on Card: _____

Signature: _____

Orders paid by check or Money Order (no cash, please) may be mailed to: Stellar Press, 634 North Grand Blvd., Suite 10 C, St. Louis, MO 63103

Please allow ten to fourteen days for delivery.

These titles and many more are available on-line at:

www.BooksOnStLouis.com